RELAT
MANIFESTO

How To Have
The Perfect Relationship

Stephen M. Whitehead

Andrews UK Limited

First published worldwide by
Andrews UK Limited
The Hat Factory
Bute Street
Luton
LU1 2EY

www.andrewsuk.com

Contents

Acknowledgements   v

About the Author   v

Foreword   vi

Chapter 1: Waking Up   1

Chapter 2: Who You Are   24

Chapter 3: Understanding Love   54

Chapter 4: Your Relationships   86

Chapter 5: Sex and Pleasure   113

Chapter 6: Togetherness   154

Chapter 7: Manifesto Rules   189

Glossary   195

Indicative Bibliography   201

For wives, lovers and friends

Acknowledgements

Special thanks to Chris Smith (Shambles Guru), Juthamard Whitehead, Catherine Chen, Anya Kingsford, Adam Dedman, Trey Dobson, Gaby Corbera, Marie Bah, Maren Peterson, Denry Machin, Ally Taylor, Anne Evandt, Sheila French, Sian Edwards, Jessica Loh, En Hudson, Emma Vanseters, Sonia Land, Crysse Morrison, Eva Pascal, Suwanna Yantraruyaha, Susan Dunsmore, Marlene Clarke, Rachel Cooper, Carlton Rounds, and all those who offered their stories for inclusion in the vignettes.

About the Author

Dr Stephen Whitehead is Visiting Professor in Gender Studies at Shih Hisn University, Taiwan and formally Senior Lecturer in Education and Gender at Keele University, UK. He has written and co-authored numerous journal articles together with ten mainstream and academic books which have been published in 17 languages. Stephen's books include, *Gender and Identity* (Oxford University Press), *The Many Faces of Men* (Random House); *Men and Masculinities* (Polity); *Masculinities Reader* (Polity); *Men, Women, Love and Romance* (Andrews); *16 Faces of Women* (Andrews); *Managing Professional Identity* (Routledge). He has been a relationship coach for over ten years and has provided guidance to hundreds of couples and individuals around the world. He lives in Chiang Mai, Thailand, with his fourth wife, Mam, and stepdaughter.

Foreword

"We cannot solve problems by using the same kind of thinking that created them."

-Albert Einstein

Whatever your gender, sexuality, age, race, or relationship experience, it is hoped this book will provide some words of empowerment and that its core message resonates for you. But don't go looking for the love myths - they are not here. Rather than rely on myths and illusion I urge each and every reader to:

> *Go out and live your life's love journey with respect, honesty, empathy, openness and confidence. Be both optimistic and strong and in turn you will not only find love, friendship and emotional comfort, you will discover yourself.*

Stephen M. Whitehead
15th September 2012

www.stephen-whitehead.com

THE RELATIONSHIP MANIFESTO

Chapter 1: Waking Up

"If you want to make your dreams to come true, the first thing you have to do is wake up" (J. M. Power)

Mary is 21 and lives in Los Angeles. She first had sex five years ago. She currently has two lovers; a man aged 19 and a divorced woman aged 32. She met her boyfriend online. Her woman lover is one of her university tutors. By the time Mary is 30 she is likely to have had sex with at least one hundred people, both male and female. If she ever does marry it is not yet clear to which sex it will be.

Susan is a barrister, aged 39. She is Singaporean, a divorcee raising two young children. Susan has dated many men since her divorce ten years ago and is currently involved with a man she met through work but who lives in Australia. They meet up three times a year. Susan occasionally sees a married male friend for what she describes as "uncomplicated fun".

Betty and Joe are married, in their early 50s. They live in the north of England. Betty and Joe are like thousands of British couples; both have jobs, their children have grown up and left home, and they have a holiday home in Spain. And every other weekend they meet other couples for swinging sex.

Welcome to 21st century relationships.

The Denial

When it comes to sex, love and romance, it appears the whole world is in a state of denial. Every wedding has become a symbol of resistance against the reality of divorce and separation, every divorce and separation the looming spectre at this feast of love.

Sex is one of the central drivers behind our very existence yet still we feel trapped between guilt and pleasure. We cling ever more desperately to the myths of Happy Ever After and when it turns out to be neither Happy or Ever After then we blame ourselves or, just as likely, our ex. Millions of us are in relationships where truths can no longer be spoken, recriminations, disappointments and regrets are mounting up, and our eyes increasingly wander to others. We stay because that is what we are expected to do, its too costly too leave, or we just don't have the emotional strength to live on our own.

Those of us who do make the move have then to cope with a social attitude which sees divorce and separation as 'failure', every ended relationship as 'failure', our inability to live the dream of eternal love as 'failure'.

That is a lot of failure.

We start out in our teens and early 20s believing the romantic novels; expecting that we will be the exception to the rule when it comes to love; yes, our love, when we find it, will be different to all the others - it will last forever.

By the time we get to our fourth and fifth decade we are wiser. But we are also bruised. We still hope, but that hope is now tinged with realism. At times it's been a very hard journey and we've felt really alone, however, along the way we've discovered who we are and who we can be. We have gotten stronger - we have matured and grown. But still society expects us to conform to some monogamous sexual model that has, for us, long ago proved inadequate. So we play along, not revealing who we truly are for fear of approbation, a critical gaze. We become hypocritical, quick to condemn the sexual behaviour of celebrities and politicians, but just as quick to emulate if the opportunity presents itself.

We either settle for being single, and learn to enjoy that state, or we remain in a relationship which eventually loses its sparkle, becomes predictable and boring, but feels safe and looks 'normal' to outsiders. And despite all this we still hold on to the myths of love and romance. Of course we ourselves cannot attain them, but we put that down to some deep inadequacy in us.

Failure, guilt, hypocrisy, shame, anger and regret - let us begin by binning these feelings altogether and facing up to the truth. Which is that you are normal, it is society that has the problem.

This book is designed to challenge your thinking on love, sex and relationships. I want to offer you not myth and illusion, but the world as it is. I am not interested in enticing you with the 'holy grail' of endless love, but the chance to be free from its myths. If you read this book and feel empowered, inspired and unshackled from whatever social constraints have been imposed on you regards sex and love, then I have achieved my aim.

I want you to stop feeling guilty at the relationship 'failures' you've had in your life. In fact I want you to stop seeing your ended relationships as any sort of failure. I want you to stop feeling guilty at desiring sex with more than one person. And I want you to stop feeling guilty at being single or if you are in a relationship, wanting to be out of it.

Whatever your age, this book is for grown-ups, not for children. The children can continue to believe the fairy tales; that is what being a child is all about. But if you still believe in the fairy tales when you are an adult then you are in denial; and living in a state of denial is not only emotionally unhealthy, it is emotionally dangerous.

Most relationships do not 'fail' they merely reach their natural conclusion - our problems arise from expecting them to go on forever

The Reality

The reality is this; if you are a man or woman aged 35 or under then you are very probably single or cohabiting. There is only a 1 in 5 chance of you being married. This is true whether you live in New York, London, Montreal, Tokyo or Shanghai. Whether you are married or not, you will have already had a number of sexual partners and been in love at least once and 'lost it'. You sustain your friendship group mostly through networking sites such as *facebook*, text messaging, and email. You have probably ventured into on-line dating with some success, but then found the love invariably peters out after a month or so. Though that didn't stop you going back to these dating sites night after night just to see 'who is on'. If you have paid employment you are working longer hours than ever before and your free time seems to be constantly under pressure. Indeed, you are finding it a challenge just to devote the time to nurturing any relationship - serious or casual. In short, life is exciting but stressful, on top of which you also realise how insecure it all is - how easily you can lose what you have. Which is one of the main reasons why you increasingly put your self first; even when you are in a relationship it doesn't occupy your every waking thought; it is not your whole life, just part of it.

If you are in your 20s or 30s, married and with children, then you do appear to be living the 'traditional romantic dream'. But does it feel like that? Maybe some of the time it does, though probably not as much as you'd like it to. And then there are those days when you do look to the future and wonder what life is going to be like when you are in your 40 or 50s. One thing you do know, you cannot take love, or your relationship, for granted.

If you are in your 50s or 60s then your life has been a bit of a roller-coaster ride when it comes to love, sex and relationships. It is highly likely you've been married, divorced, - perhaps several times - and had more sexual partners than you care to remember.

As they say, you've 'lived a little'. But then you look around you and so have your friends.

And what about the 40-something woman and man? Well, this decade is arguably the one that will come to define your life. This generation is, nowadays, at its most creative, sexual, independent, and confident. It is also potentially at its most stressed. So much going on, so much done and yet so much still to do, it makes for a heady time; juggling more roles than you can count and having high expectations of all of them. However, more and more of this generation are doing it on their own; separated, divorced, or life-long singles, often childless and happy about that, or long-time single parents. Again, for millions of 40-somethings, their lifestyle is a zillion miles away from their teenage 'reality'.

So can we define the love and relationship reality that is common to most if not all of us? Yes we can. The reality is that we are each of us on a 'love journey' and in one way or another it will last throughout our lives. This love journey will have many twists and turns, some days it will run slow, other days it will be racing along. On occasion it will feel like a stroll, other times an emotional and arduous trek. Do not fear the journey and do not seek to avoid it. Embrace its uniqueness and do not expect it to be smooth everyday of your life. That is just not going to happen. Neither should you expect to share this love journey with anyone else. It is yours alone - others have their own journey to experience. The journey is everything - it has no end - it is constant movement through your life. Value the flow and energy of it, and the fact you will reach no final destination - like love itself, the love journey is an ongoing experience, not a final and unchangeable state.

That is the reality. What about the myths?

The Myths

Myths are fictions, not facts. They are what we hope, imagine and idealize, but too often mistake as real. Life is full of them. We are full of them. In fact it is hard to live without them. Myths are stories we've been told, we tell ourselves and in turn pass on to others; they are fantasised misrepresentations of reality but they are highly seductive.

When it comes to sex, love and relationships, myths abound. Here are nine of the most persistent 'love myths'.

1. Marriages are for ever.

2. Strong relationships must always be based on love.

3. I need someone special in my life if I am to be happy

4. If I love someone then it is for life.

5. Romance makes a relationship.

6. My past relationships failed because of me.

7. My past relationships failed because of my ex's.

8. If my partner is unfaithful then s/he doesn't love me.

9. Sex is only ever good with a partner we love.

A key objective of this book is to firstly help you recognise these myths and the power they continue to have over us, understanding how they still grip our imaginations and aspirations, and secondly, to then let them go. Only at that point can we go on to reach our ultimate goal and the aim of this book; which is to give you the courage and guidance to live a life of guilt-free multiple relationships - some casual, some serious, some memorable, some not, but everyone of which you can learn from, every one of which will help you grow as an individual.

We hold on to love myths so as to avoid reality. We should save the love myths for where they belong - Walt Disney cartoons

The Consequences

Imagine a world where children are constantly told these nine love myths, having them reinforced through fairly tales, romantic sagas, 'Happy Ever After' stories, religious ideology and moral codes. In effect, a value system is imposed on the children regards 'true love relationships' which stays with them all their lives. But then the world turns out not to be like the myths at all. It is very different. It is harder, more complex, more changeable, and certainly less predictable. The children grow up believing in the myths but then find their adult lives to be not myth-like whatsoever. Consequently, they can easily feel let down, guilty, inadequate, confused.

Now imagine this child to be you - because it is. You may not be a child, but you still feel a strong urge to hold on to child-like myths. Why? Because they are comforting. Despite your experiences of life, love and relationships you want to continue to believe in the myths; they may be fairy tales but part of you wants to take them as real. So hold on to them you do, grasping them ever more tightly even in the face of the relationship reality unfolding around you.

But eventually the myths cannot be sustained. You have to let them go and at this point you may well do something very radical. Having come to accept the illusion behind the myths of love you do a complete about turn and grasp at another myth -the 10th one.

10. There is no one in this life for me.

You fall back on this 10th myth out of fear of being hurt or rejected again; disappointment at love, and recognition that, in the end, you need to protect yourself. While this is perfectly understandable you need to know that the 10th myth is the most dangerous of them all. Again, this is one of the myths that this book seeks to debunk.

Relationships nourish us - the more we have the more we grow

The Awakening

Regardless of our age, gender or sexuality, we are all lovers at different times in our lives. Every one of us, during our lifetime, connects intimately with someone, usually more than one person, and in such a forceful way that it changes us. It can be a wonderful, if highly emotive, experience - its one of the thrills and advantages of being a mature, sexually active, man or woman. However, intimate connections are not only about pleasure and excitement, they are also about personal growth - through our most profound and intense love relationships so we develop as adults. The problem is, we are bombarded with messages about 'the one', and 'relationships for life'. How realistic is this today?

Like many people I have undertaken a search of my family tree. It was fairly easy to go back to the mid 1800s and find my distant ancestors. On my mother's side they come from Liverpool, on my father's side, from Pateley Bridge, Yorkshire, so very much northern British. There were some differences in profession and class, but one commonality amongst both sets of families - there were many children born. In one instance, nine children were born to my great, great, great grandparents who lived in the

Yorkshire Dales. That couple were married when they were both in their early 20s, they died in their late 70s, so a long life. And during that half-century of living together as husband and wife they produced nine children.

Back then this lifestyle was typical - generation after generation expecting there to be just one person whom they met around the age of 20, got married shortly afterwards, and lived together without ever contemplating separation or divorce. It really was a 'till death us do part' relationship. However, the gay or lesbian person stayed quiet, in the background, hiding their sexuality from prying eyes. The unfaithful partner also covered their tracks. The dysfunctional family stuck it out regardless. No one got divorced. Whether they liked it or not, everyone had to live the myth, at least in some ways, though whether they did much personal growing is another question altogether.

Today is much different. We have choices our grandparents did not. We have the contraceptive pill, we have education, we have employment possibilities, we have technology, and we have globalisation. We live in changing times, and these times have transformed the way we experience love and relationships. The world has changed, people have changed with it; unfortunately the myths of love have not. They were written for a different era, one long gone. So we need a new perspective on love, sex and romance. We need to be realistic about long-term relationships and how to handle them. We have to wake up to the reality of modern love.

Awakening is vital to 21st century relationship living. We may still yearn for a traditional partnership, but the fact is we are no longer living in a traditional world. Not only are our lives different; our expectations of what life has to offer us are vastly different from previous generations. At the same time our quest for love remains as constant as it always has. Unfortunately, this quest for a 'pure love relationship' is now in direct conflict with the reality of 21st century lifestyles and expectations.

The only people who have anything to fear from 10 year renewable relationship vows are the divorce lawyers

Post-marriage Society

Globally, the institution of marriage appears in real trouble. It is not exactly dead, but it is in intensive care. In the US, half of all marriages now end in divorce, likewise in parts of Canada, notably Quebec. Across Europe the divorce rate varies between 30% and 55%, with the highest rates being in Scandinavia and the lower rates in Italy and Ireland. Singapore, Thailand and Taiwan are typical of Southeast Asian countries in that they have seen their divorce rates double in just a few years. In China the divorce rate has been rising at 20% a year for the past decade. Even India, which has historically had very low levels of divorce, is seeing increases; Kerala, one of the most educationally advanced states in India has experienced a 350% increase in divorce over the last ten years. Few if any countries are seeing their marriage rate rising; what they are seeing is their divorce rates go up year on year.

At time of writing, Prince William and Kate Middleton, the British royal family couple, are about to get married. Their wedding will be viewed by billions of people worldwide. The vast majority of those watching will wish Kate and William a long and happy life together without ever separating or divorcing. However, the odds are stacked against it. In The British royal family is no more immune from the dramatic changes that have occurred in relationships over the past half-century than any other family. Like most families, they too have had their share of splits, infidelities, scandal, divorces and re-marriages. Sure, we may enjoy the spectacle of Kate and William's marriage, and indulge in the fairy tale romance of it all, but the relationship path awaiting them has even more potholes in it than it has for the rest of us.

Despite the international popularity of a British Royal Wedding, all the evidence shows that marriage is going out of fashion, and virtually every couple that does get married tests the waters by living together first. In the 1950s only 10% of British couples cohabited before marriage, now over 95% do, that is if they get married at all. More of us are living alone, without any partner. In the UK, the percentage of singletons has doubled since 1970, to 12% of the adult population. By 2030 it is estimated that 46% of British men and 45% of British women, will be unmarried. Not surprisingly, these changes are impacting on births. In the UK, 45% of births are now outside marriage. In the 1970s it was 10%. In parts of Canada and the US, 60% of births are now to single parents or cohabiting couples.

While more of us are living as singletons it doesn't follow that we are having less sex. Men and women in their 50s and 60s are now recognised by US and European sexual health agencies as one of the high risk groups for STDs; they are enjoying freedom from pregnancy, any children have left home, and they are embracing internet dating with enthusiasm. Despite the heightened criminalisation of the profession in many countries, more men of all age groups are visiting sex workers, while increasing numbers of single women visit countries such as Gambia and Jamaica for similar fun. While sex surveys are notoriously difficult to substantiate, it is clear that by the time they get to 40, most Western men and women will have had at least 10, and in many instances lots more, sexual partners.

All the evidence suggests that the younger generation, by the time they reach 40 will be even more sexually experienced than current 40-somethings. For example, around the world, the average age at which a teenager now first has sex is 16; in some countries it is 14. The percentage of teenage girls in the West who are sexually active has quadrupled over the last 50 years. The same trends are evident in every developed and developing country. Everywhere one looks teenagers are losing their virginity at younger and younger ages. In the past, women especially delayed sex until marriage. In 1970 the average age at first marriage for US women was 21. In 1970 only 36% of US women aged 20 to 24 had never been married. By 2000, that had doubled to 73%.

Even in highly patriarchal and conservative countries, such as Pakistan and India, where families put a premium on virginity, increasing numbers of teenagers are not delaying sex until marriage. They just have oral and anal sex instead. Millions of such teenagers are only virgins 'technically'. By the time they get to 18, most teenagers today will have had several sexual partners. And they are continuing to have them through their 20s and onwards. What they are not doing is getting married and they are certainly not staying celibate.

While childhood is shortening, adulthood is lengthening. Taken globally, the life expectancy for all people is now 67. In developed countries it is 77 and rising. In the early 20th century, life expectancy in the US and UK was just 47. A 25 year old today can reasonably expect to live for at least another 55 years, and for most of that time they will be sexually active, starting from their early teens. That 25 year old will already have had a number of sexual partners, and they will go on to have many more.

A 16 year old living today in a developed country has a one in four chance of living to 100 and a 4 out of 5 chance of never being married. How many sexual partners do you imagine they will have over 100 years?

All this suggests very strongly that we are now at the beginnings of what will come to be recognised as the post-marriage society, where even the 10% or so of younger people who do venture down the aisle have a 50% chance or more of walking to the divorce courts a decade or so later; where fewer and fewer of us even bother getting married, preferring to remain as cohabiting couples, 'living-apart-togethers' (LAT's) or just freelancing singles. Under these circumstances the notion of 'till death us do part' is not only meaningless it is positively mythical. Romantic, everlasting love becomes an aspiration that few of us can hold on to for long. Maybe we never could, the point is that holding on to such myths in the 21st century carries real risks of guilt, feelings of failure, disappointment, bitterness, low self-esteem, regret, even depression. This is mental baggage that we just don't need.

Which is precisely why we require a new Relationship Manifesto, one written for the 21st century, not the 19th. We need to recognise what is happening around us and revise our understandings of what it means to be in a relationship, and even what 'long-term' means. In this book I suggest that long-term means ten years. Why ten? Because 7.5 years is the average length of time of all 'committed' relationships between adults; marriages, cohabitations, 'LATS'; in which case 10 years is making a commitment to go that extra distance.

We need to stop holding on to myths which are long past their sell-by date, and instead embrace the world as it is, not as it is in Walt Disney land, as it might have been for our grandparents, or as we assumed it was when we were children.

This new world is not a bad place to be; it is not negative just because we are having more serial loves during our lifetimes. Every ended relationship is not another 'failure' to look back on with regret and bitterness. We are not promiscuous just because we have had sex with many people; in fact I urge you to disregard the word 'promiscuous' altogether. When it comes to sex, you decide, not society. You may be living alone today, but don't assume that is an inevitable state. It is not. If you look for them, people will come into your life regularly, some will stay a long time, some not. Whatever, we will learn from every experience and that, ultimately, is the point of it. As I go on to explain, there are real positive possibilities for each of us in all these changes.

By reading this book it is hoped you will be released from endlessly toting negative feelings and emotional baggage from relationship to relationship. At which point you can then get on with enjoying relationships to the full; being in them, being out of them, and being in between them. You will have recognised the love relationship reality around you, accepted it, and then moved on to fully embrace what comes next in your own life's 'love journey'.

Promises of fidelity invariably turn us into liars

Living with Change

It is not just the evidence for changing love relationships that is overwhelming, gender roles themselves are changing - what it means to be a man or a woman is a whole lot different from even 25 years ago. Sex and sexual identity have, similarly, undergone enormous transformations in just two decades. Don't imagine the 'swinging sixties' were about sexual freedom, they were not. Well, they may have been about some men's sexual freedom, but the fact is it wasn't until the 1990s that we started to see the really important and profound shift - in women's sense of gender and sexual identity.

Do you know the most dramatic social change of the 20th century? It was the emancipation of women. Some might attribute this to feminism. I attribute it to globalisation and the universal awakening of women that accompanied it. Over a period of 100 years, 50% of the world's population changed their outlook on life. The 21 year old woman who entered the 20th century has little in common with the 21 year old woman who left it. We are only now beginning to see the consequences of this dramatic identity shift as it still has a long way to go, but for sure women, globally, will exert more power in this century than any century since.

It is fine me telling you what I think and what I have discovered through my research. In the end, you have to make your own mind up and decide what works for you in terms of love relationships, and at different times in your life. No one book can provide all the answers for all 6.5 billion people. What this book does is give you with a much fuller and more accurate understanding of what makes and breaks a modern relationship; it helps you appreciate that your life is fine without a big love relationship to define it; and will empower you in all your relationships, the long term ones, and the casual.

So to reinforce my points, I include throughout the book vignettes from my research; examples of women and men who illustrate through their own lives and experiences what is happening, worldwide, in terms of changing love, sex and relationships. Here are five of them:

Susan

Susan is British and 55 years old. She is fit and very attractive. She has two grown up children from her marriage, which lasted 28 years, until her divorce five years ago. Throughout her marriage she was a devoted wife and mother, always putting the family first. Then at the age of 45 she got the urge to go back to university, this time to do a PhD. The next few years were an emotional and intellectual rollercoaster for Susan. She changed, grew in confidence, became more questioning, and independent. The PhD was more than just studying and research; it was Susan discovering her possibilities outside of motherhood and married life. Her husband, however, found this new assertive Susan rather problematic. Towards the end of Susan's PhD, they separated and subsequently divorced. Susan became a university lecturer. In many respects, Susan is now the woman she always wanted to be but because of social and family constraints, couldn't. She has regular boyfriends though won't commit exclusively to any man until she is sure they are able to accept her as she is, the woman she has become.

Berit

Berit is 41, Swedish and bisexual. She got married at 25 and that relationship lasted five years and produced one child. Since then, she has had numerous affairs, with both men and women, the longest of which, with a woman, lasted eight years. Apart from her marriage, she has always lived as a single person. She and her daughter now live in Stockholm where Berit works as a project manager for a multi-national company. If you ask Berit why her marriage ended, she will tell you it felt "too restricting". Although she'd had little experience of bi-sexuality prior to her marriage, Berit had always felt some sexual attraction towards women. At the same time, she likes the company and sexual presence of men. By the time she was in her late 20s, she was anxious to explore the duality of her sexual identity. Berit has been in love three times in her life. The first time with her ex-husband, then again with another man with whom she had a brief but very intense relationship, and lastly Asa, the woman with whom she had the eight-year affair. At the moment Berit is not seeing anyone. Her work is demanding and she is happy to devote her private time to her 13 year old daughter. Berit is confident, a strong personality and someone who has very clear ideas of what she likes and does not like. She is uncomfortable with the idea of sexual exclusivity and has come to realise that monogamy not for her. Whoever comes into her life in the future, Berit is very clear they will need to accept both her personality and her sexual life-style.

Mike

Mike is 37, American and gay. He lives in New York where he works in marketing. He is an attractive man and has had many sexual encounters since his early teens, and some big love affairs. He has always been comfortable with his sexuality and enjoys a supportive relationship with his parents and family members. He has tried sex with women, but finds it unsatisfactory. Seven years ago Mike met Raul, a 35 year old Latin-American male. They made initial contact through a gay online dating agency and shortly afterwards decided to live together in New York. A year later, in 2005, they got married in Massachusetts, the first US state to legalize same-sex marriage. Mike and Raul recognise that they love each other but also that there are times when they may wish to have sex with other men. So from the outset of their marriage they have had an agreement that monogamy is not a central feature of their relationship. When they do have sex with others it is with the knowledge and approval of each other. Their marriage is strong; they trust each other, are open and honest, and they are very happy.

Victor

Victor is French and aged 21. He comes from an educated, middle class, Parisian family. He is studying economics and politics at university and hopes for a career with a major corporation. However, his main leisure interest at the moment is devising online games and creating websites for his friends. Victor has a wide circle of friends, especially women. He started dating girls when he was 13 and first had sex at 14. Over the past seven years, Victor has had sex with over 20 women, mostly younger or the same age as him, though three were several years older. Victor's mother and father divorced four years ago. His elder brother (aged 35) is also divorced, and his younger sister (aged 18) has already had several serious relationships. Victor lives away from home and during holidays shares his time between his mother and father. His father has a woman partner who lives with him, and his mother regularly dates men. Victor has no plans to 'settle down' with any one woman, and his female friends don't push this expectation onto him. Like him, they are not sure what their plans are after university, though going and living abroad is certainly one option that many are seriously pursuing. Victor accepts that other lovers will come into his life in the future but right now he has no intention of ever getting married.

Lin

Lin is a 32 year old Taiwanese woman. She is single, and lives alone in an upmarket condo in the heart of Taipei. She works as a senior manager in a large mobile phone manufacturing company. Lin comes from a traditional Taiwanese family and as such she respects her parents and tries to follow the path they would like for her. However, she is also very much a global citizen. She has travelled all over the world, both for holidays and work. She speaks excellent English and some German. She has never been married but had lots of boyfriends, some serious. She first had sex when she was 17, and been in love three times in her life so far. Her latest boyfriend is Giovanni, a 43 year old Italian who lives in Turin. She met Giovanni through an online dating agency and after three months of regular email contact they decided to meet. Lin flew to Italy to spend two weeks with Giovanni during which time she met his family and children (Giovanni has two teenage children from his first marriage). In a few weeks time, Giovanni flies to Taipei to spend his summer holidays with Lin. Lin is looking forward to his visit very much indeed. However, where the relationship goes from *here she is not at all sure, though she is happy just to be in it for the moment.*

The five vignettes are all different in their detail, but with a strong commonality. That is, the sense of independence and freedom from traditional values which the individuals are exhibiting. Victor is typical of males his age, education and class; they are connected to the global network and living very free lifestyles, as are their parents. Mike and Raul are increasingly typical of gay couples in the West, many of whom are rewriting their marriage vows to reflect a new reality, one far removed from the dichotomy of faithfulness-infidelity. The three women have all experienced 'big love' but also travelled a path that has at times taken them well away from the expectations of traditional romantic relationships. It is not that the women completely deny the possibility of or desire for a big romantic relationship, its just that they have other aspects of their lives which they want to protect, not least their strong and assertive femininity, their independence and their wish for a relationship which is sexually satisfying, emotionally fulfilling and built on equality. These women, when they do get into a committed relationship, are making very rational judgements about what they expect from it and what they expect from their partner.

There is another important aspect that is common to all of these individuals, and will be common in your life also. That is, there is change and movement - nothing is constant, nothing is predictable. Accepting this fluidity, and not being fazed by it, is crucial for understanding and being in, 21st century relationships.

Finally, none of the adult women has had the 'perfect relationship'; they may have hoped for such a relationship when they were teenagers, but they eventually had to be honest with themselves about what they wanted from life and what they were prepared to put into a relationship. Also, none of them has had a 'failed' relationship. They have learnt and grown from every romantic and sexual encounter, however brief, however long-lasting. Importantly, they are still changing. They have had times in their lives when they wanted and sought commitment with one person, and times in their lives when they wanted something 'extra.' But the ultimate commitment is to their selves. And that takes honesty, self-knowledge, and courage.

From China to India, from the USA to the UK, women are the ones instigating divorce not men, they are the ones avoiding marriage altogether; they are the ones rewriting the rulebook on relationships. Women know that society is not going to judge them negatively if they are single, divorced or cohabiting. If they decide to bring children up as single parents or not have children at all, then they see that as their choice.

Women's increasing expectation of an independent life style, which may or may not involve different relationships at different times, is now firmly embedded in modern life.

Being loved is not a constitutional right - we have to earn it

The Paradox of Love

All these changes open doors, however the more open doors we face then the more uncertain we can feel. At this point we then confront the paradox of love.

Wanting love is perfectly natural. Humans have always sought love relationships. However, in the past societies were organised very differently. There were distinct roles for men and distinct roles for women, and rarely did they cross over. Consequently, romantic love and relationships were built around these apparent stable structures and the family life that ensued. This all produced a sense of order and continuity. Life seemed predictable, settled, and functional. And in many ways it was, though we should not look back on the past with any great nostalgia. After all, life might have been ordered in terms of gender roles, but LGBT people were excluded from this tidy social system; millions of women died in childbirth; life expectancy was short; and just surviving day to day was a major challenge. It still is for millions around the world.

The myths of love were embedded in this gender structure, where men went out to work and women stayed home and raised the family. However, women, despite the persistence of the love myths, in reality got married as much out of social and economic necessity as out of passion. They had little choice if they were to survive in a world run by men and built around patriarchal stereotypes, values and attitudes.

Nowadays, it is just as likely that the woman is earning as much as her partner, and has better career prospects. She can choose to have sex with whom she likes. She can move in and out of relationships freely, without social stigma. She is living a life of independence beyond the dreams of her female ancestors. Why, then, would she get married? Its not for economic security - if she is middle class and educated then she can acquire that herself. No, the reason why women move into relationships today is for love, for the feeling of emotional intimacy and for sexual desire. Having children may also be on the agenda, but then millions of women are having children outside of relationships. Again, we are seeing how changing gender identities and expectations are creating a whole new world.

The paradox is, we still yearn for lifetime love, but we cannot hold on to it. We seek love, but do not relish the feeling of emotional risk and exposure that comes with it. We want 'the one' in our life, but on our terms - we are only prepared to compromise so much. And we place so much expectation on love when we do feel we've found it that it almost buckles under the weight.

No one goes into a full on love relationship, commits to this, but plans to be out of it in a few years. However, that is a reality we have to be prepared for.

Our expectations have not caught up with the facts. When we imagine love and romance we still conjure up the Walt Disney cartoon version, where a stereotypically heterosexual couple overcome hardship through true love and commitment and ultimately go on to live Happily Ever After. Of course, they never have to worry about the kids and their education, paying the mortgage, holding down a job, credit cards and debt, the in-laws, sexual dysfunctionality and attractions to others outside of marriage.

Millions of people are trapped between the myths and the reality, and the one time a year this becomes so apparent is Christmas. This festivity is when we are all meant to 'be happy', be together, and be with family and friends. The expectations of 'Happy Christmas' are colossal, and insidious. The whole purpose (apart from spending) is to validate family life, our love for our partner, prove we are 'ok', even if the rest of the year its not. Consequently, Christmas has degenerated into a living hell for many couples, divorcees, and especially single people. It has lost whatever attractions it once had and instead has become the festive season of debt, dread and disappointment. The stress toll on individuals and families during Christmas is immense, as much research shows.

The hard truth is we can choose to continue along the path of paradoxical love, reinforced by myths of happy ever after but always left with a feeling of failure and dissatisfaction when the reality turns out to be somewhat different, or we can face up to the way we are actually living, and experiencing life. For sure, unless we do wake up then we cannot fully grow up. We will remain forever rooted to the world of childhood romantic myths. Like Christmas, these myths might work for children, but they are misleading if not downright dangerous in adulthood.

The book

Over the next six chapters I will to take you deeper into the world of modern love relationships. Along the way I am going to explore your identity and how you can create it like our own unique work of art. I am going to describe the different types of love and the five main relationship types that most of us experience at least once in our lives. I will explore sex and pleasure, their importance to our wellbeing and how to embrace them without guilt. And I will take you into the realms of togetherness, being with someone in such a way as to give your love relationship the best possible chance of a long life. Finally, I reveal the Manifesto Rules and the Relationship Vows for modern relationships.

Chapter 2: Who You Are

"Never be bullied into silence. Never allow yourself to be made a victim. Accept no one's definition of your life; define yourself" (Harvey Feinstein)

To better understand how relationships work, and flounder, we have to first understand the key component that goes into relationships - us. Who we are, who we have been, and who we might become, these are fundamental to our constantly evolving relationships with others. If you profess to love someone you presumably love their identity. The same goes for those who love us. So how does this identity of ours evolve and can we change it? Is it fixed and constant or is it fluid and variable?

In this chapter I reveal how our identity reacts to external stimuli, also how we can make changes to our identity if we are minded to do so. Sure, we can imagine we have no power over our identity; our character and personality. But this is not true. Our actions and thoughts emerge out of the social world we inhabit; they are validated and reinforced through culture - ritual and routine. But these can change - we can change them. As I go on to explain, we have more power over our identity than we might think. At the same time, this power is not total, not absolute - there are limits.

It is also important to recognise that there is not just one identity in every relationship, there are three; you, your partner and, arising from the interactions of both of you, the third identity, that of the relationship itself. This highlights the fact that every relationship you have will be different in many ways; there may be patterns but no two relationships are alike for the simple reason that all of us are different, each couple is different. Which is why each relationship is unique also.

Finally, we have to recognise that all sexual relationships are ultimately about gender - femininity and masculinity - and how we think and act as men and women. This is just as true of same sex relationships as it is of hetero relationships. In this chapter I describe how gender identity has profoundly changed for women over the past few decades, and the different ways men are responding to women's new expression of femininity. To emphasise these significant transformations I draw on case studies from my research - many different types of men and women from around the world.

My identity is just like yours - it is work in progress

Identity Work

You are not your genitalia

Dai was born in 1983 to Vietnamese/American parents. She has lived in San Francisco all her life. Long before the onset of puberty Dai knew she was different. Born as an intersexed person, Dai had both male and female genitalia. She could have been raised as either male or female, but her family chose male. Dai's mind, however, rejected that label, preferring to be female. And so, at the age of 16, Dai began to present herself as overtly female. She had hormone treatment and, at the age of 22, went to Thailand for genital replacement surgery. Dai is now a she, in every respect.

Ever since she had the capacity to think for herself Dai has been on a journey of discovery and creation. She has been discovering and creating her gender and sexual identity. This has touched every aspect of her being, especially sex, love and relationships. Sexually, Dai is a 'tom'; that is a lesbian who is attracted to more feminine women. She has a female partner, Kay, whom she has lived with for two years. She is hoping that one day she and Kay can have children.

Dai might seem different to most people, but the fact is she is not. In one important respect she is just like you and I; she has engaged in identity work; creating herself using the identity kit she was born with and adding in all the additional elements of culture, ethnicity, age, class, education and upbringing. The difference is that Dai has had to do more identity work than most of us. She has had to work more explicitly at creating her self than most of us have to, the reason being that she was given a sex identity that was out of kilter with her mindset.

There are millions of intersexed people like Dai around the world, in the UK alone it is estimated there are over 30,000. Some are straight, some are gay, some are bi, some are transgendered, some transsexual. All are unique.

But they are no more unique than you. They just appear so because society finds it hard to accept those who do not fit comfortably into the sex/gender binary of distinct male-female identities.

Dai gives us a direct insight into the realities of identity. She, like all of us, is on a pathway of self-creation. There are some signposts to help us in this process, but ultimately who we are is significantly down to us.

Not only is our identity largely created by us, it is also in constant flux. That is, it changes as we age, as we experience life, and especially as we experience love, sex and relationships. We might call this 'growing up', but the truth is we don't stop growing once we reach 21. It carries on throughout our life.

Do not imagine who you are today is who you were five years ago, or who you will be in five years time. You have changed over time and will continue to change in many ways, some overtly, some subtle and less obvious. All this renders you unique amongst the 6.5 billion people who inhabit this planet, just like me.

This is identity as a process, not an outcome. We may have a particular set of genitalia, hormones, DNA, which is almost identical to everyone else, yet despite this we still come out being different to everyone else in terms of who we are and how we live our lives. None of it is predictable.

There is artistry to this identity work that is important to recognise, if not to celebrate. That is, whether we realise it or not, each of us is in a process of constant and often imaginative, self-creation; whether it is changing our appearance through dress, our bodies at the gym, our knowledge through education, our skills through work, or our cultural awareness through travel. Who we choose to associate with, who we choose to work with, who we choose to sleep with, who we choose to live with, these will all influence who we are today and who we may be tomorrow.

Because we are living so much longer, experiencing multiple relationships and as I go on to explain in Chapter 4, different types of relationships, so we should recognise what this means for us as individuals, and for our love life. But in order to appreciate what is happening with us, to us, we first have to discard the idea that biology is destiny; in particular we must reject the ideologies that, for whatever reason, seek to perpetuate ethnic, racial, ageist, gender and sexual stereotypes. In this age of globalisation, when we are living with so much diversity around us, then stereotypes are particularly unhelpful; they do no justice to the complexity of human nature, and of our brains.

Our brains are powerful machines which none of us use to their maximum potential. They respond to external stimuli; to their environment, to language, to image. Our brains process information - they create reality for us, they create our minds. Our IQ, for instance, can be increased through motivational techniques, training, discipline, meditation, reading, exposure to alternative ways of thinking and being. Fundamentally, a female brain is no different to a male's. The brain does not emerge innately understanding how to behave as a man or woman - this is learned; though in most instances it is primed towards a particular sexuality from conception. Though, again, how this sexuality is then expressed as individual practice is more a cultural issue than a biological one. In terms of gender (how we live our lives as men and women), the brain is completely neutral. A man's brain is not hardwired to hunt bison in the wilderness, but it can be trained to hunt money in Manhattan. A woman's brain does not contain a 'maternity clock', though it can be taught how to raise and nurture children. Similarly, a woman can be the hunter, while a man can be the nurturer. There are no biological, or identity, barriers to this - only cultural ones.

You are unique but not original. You are the total accumulation of all your life's interactions, as we all are

What we think is true and what we assume is reality, is limited by our exposure to knowledge and difference. In particular, who we are can be limited by where we are. You may be a true blue liberal in New York, but in Wyoming you will likely be a flaming Republican. You may be raised as a fundamentalist Muslim in Pakistan, but more likely you'll be a fundamentalist Mormon in Utah. If you are born in Thailand there is a 95% chance you are Buddhist, but if you are born in Italy there a 95% likelihood of you being Catholic.

So the baby Thai is given a Buddhist identity whether he/she likes it or not, just as the baby Italian is given a Catholic one. But then the Italian can visit Thailand and convert to Buddhism, while the Thai can visit the Vatican and convert to Christianity. It is all down to exposure to new knowledge and to the choices we then make as adults.

Identity is not something, therefore, that is imposed upon us from birth and from which we have no escape. It is not fixed throughout our lifetime; it is not hardwired into us from conception. Identity is a complex and dynamic process of being an individual in the social worlds we inhabit. It is a mix of nature and nurture, but with a much heavier influence on the nurture than the nature. Who our parents are and where they live is, undoubtedly, the most influential factor on whom we grow up to become. But this factor lessens in influence as we mature. In the age of globalisation, with its advanced technology, information systems, international travel, educational opportunities, and social networking, identity is more fluid and flexible than it has ever been. The sex we are born, the language we speak, any religion we are born into, and our experiences through childhood, these are just some of the major influences on our identity. But none of these are inevitably stable or determined. We cannot predict how a person will think and behave on the basis of whether they have a penis or a vagina; speak English or speak Mandarin; follow Islam or Christianity; are raised in a nuclear family or a single parent one.

Although you and I were born into distinct social and cultural settings, we both know that we have made decisions on how to live our life countless times over the years. We have made choices over friendships, family, education, career, sex and relationships. For sure, people living in more open cultures and societies enjoy more choice than those living in closed and traditional ones, nevertheless, exercising choice is increasingly a characteristic, if not expectation, of human experience.

Choice is not evenly spread for every man, woman and child in the world. Clearly, money, class, culture and a host of over factors all kick in to increase our options or reduce them. But for rapidly growing numbers of us, especially those born since the end of the 2nd World War, choices have multiplied. This is one of the main reasons why marriages are down, divorces are up, and singleton lifestyles increasingly common; and the sex that has largely driven these transformations and experienced the most opening up of choice in their lives has been the female one.

Do not leave it too long to discover who you can be

Changing Women

It may have been a man's world once, but not any longer

Jemma is a thirty year-old Canadian woman. She is a lawyer in a large Toronto law firm. Jemma's family is quite traditional, but Jemma is not. She first had sex at age sixteen, and has had many sexual partners since. During her early twenties she had a big love relationship that lasted for five years, however this broke up because her partner wanted marriage and children, but she did not. She is currently without a partner. She has no intention of having children, at least before she is well established in her career. She has tried soft drugs, but now doesn't even smoke. She likes to travel, party, and spend time with her friends, who include gay men and women - singletons like her - and some married couples. Jemma likes men but is realistic about what she wants out of life. She is a regular user of online dating sites and usually has sex with a man on the second date. Like most of her female friends, Jemma will have sex when it suits her and doesn't see it as condition of love. However, she is always open to the possibility of a full-on love relationship, but not if it means compromising her independent lifestyle and career ambitions. Whoever she does eventually 'settle down' with, Jemma will insist on a relationship of equality, even if she and her partner have very different roles.

There are millions of 'Jemma's' now around the world; you will know some, you may even be one. In fact they are so numerous that you might wonder why I have put her in this book. Well, precisely because she so clearly illustrates the change in women over the past five decades.

Here is another example of what I term, sociologically, the 'postmodern woman':

Zhu is a 34 year old Chinese woman. She lives in Shanghai where she works as a senior Human Resource manager for an international company. Zhu is single and lives alone in a modern high-rise condominium in Pudong, one of the quieter parts of the city. Zhu's family still live in Chengdu, central China, far from Shanghai, though she tries to visit them each Chinese New Year holiday. Zhu has not had many relationships through her life, though she is now dating an older man, a divorcee aged 45. He is doctor in a local hospital. Financially, Zhu is very comfortable. Her salary has increased steadily since she started her career and she is gradually increasing her professional status. She drives a new Volkswagen, eats out at fine restaurants and has acquired a taste for wine. She takes a yearly holiday skiing in Haerbin, northern China and has travelled all over southeast Asia and to Europe and America. Zhu is one year into a part-time, distance learning MBA at Hong Kong university. She has many friends and a large network of people she keeps in contact with through email and 'renren', the Chinese equivalent of facebook. Zhu often feels torn between the more traditional expectations and values of her family, and her independent, financially secure lifestyle in Shanghai. Her family admire her success, though they also hope that one day she will marry and have a child.

Physically, Jemma and Zhu are living at different points of the globe but culturally they are like sisters. And you can find women just like them in every developed and developing country. Globalisation is clearly the over-arching dynamic which is bringing change for women like Jemma and Zhu, but within this lies the all- important factor of education. Both are university graduates, both are singletons, both have careers, neither have children, and both have had sexual experiences with more than one man. But it is their advanced education that has set the foundations for their lifestyle. This is the means by which they have become middle class.

The middle classes are booming globally. According to a 2010 report by *The Economist* more than half the world's population is middle class for the first time in history. When my grandmother was born, in 1900, 5% of world's population was middle class, now it is close to 60% and rising.

People are buying refrigerators and televisions on credit in the slums of Sao Paulo. 3 million Chinese now ski in a country that didn't offer the sport 15 years ago. Sales of quality wine are booming in China and Hong Kong, as are sales of Mercedes and BMW cars in India - that country alone will see its middle class rise from 5% in 2005 to over 40% by 2025.

None of these social changes are possible without positive change in the status of women. As the World Bank stipulated in 2007, no country can aspire to prosperity if 50% of its population (women) are uneducated and marooned in poverty. Women are the key, the essential element, if a country is to develop. And around the world, women are proving this mantra.

- In Hong Kong, women now occupy 30% of management positions, up from 15% in 1992.

- In the UK, women now own over 50% of the nation's wealth, growing to 60% by 2040. In the USA 51% of the nation's wealth is owned by women, as are 89% of all US bank accounts.

- More than half the world's richest women are Chinese. 30% of Maserati's Chinese buyers are women.

- Across the EU, 40% of company directors are women, while the Asia-Pacific region has the highest percentage of women in senior management globally - 27%; the Philippines has the highest level of women in management at 56%.

- In the EU, since 2000, women have filled 6 million of the 8 million jobs created.

- Women have outnumbered men in the Canadian workforce since 2007. In January 2010, the same shift happened in the USA with 800,000 more women than men on payrolls. American women are not only picking up more work, men are losing work more rapidly than women, a trend that is accelerated with each economic downturn.

- Women may soon become the majority breadwinners in the USA, given the rising number of long-term unemployed men and the ever-rising share of women-headed households. Currently, two-thirds of American homes have women as the main provider, or co-provider.

- Two-thirds of the 11 million jobs lost in the USA since the 2008 recession were jobs held by men. Indeed, Larry Summers, economic advisor to Barack Obama, recently stated; "when the economy recovers five years from now, one in six men who are aged 25-54 will not be working".

- Economists anticipate that by 2024, the average Western woman will be earning more money than the average Western man. Already in the UK, young women professionals are now earning more than their male counterparts a trend that is also occurring in the US.

- In Brazil, India, China and the UAE, over 75% of women want to hold a top job. 89% of women in India describe themselves as 'very ambitious'.

- Worldwide, women will fill 13 of the 15 job categories that will develop the most over the next ten years.

- Until as recently as 1991, Switzerland still had voting restrictions for women, however, in 2010 Swiss women outnumbered men in government for the first time. At time of writing, Switzerland now joins with countries such as Australia, Bangladesh, Finland, Iceland, Peru, Brazil, Argentina, India, Germany, Ireland, Costa Rica and Kosovo in having a female president or prime minister.

- A 2011 study by Mastercard Worldwide which measured women's socio-economic advancement, shows them making significant progress globally, not least in highly patriarchal countries such as Saudi Arabia, the UAE, Qatar, Kuwait, Lebanon and Egypt.

The gender issue for the 21st century will not be the emancipation of women, but what to do with the men who are left behind

These gender changes are happening slower in some countries than others, but the indisputable fact is that women, just as with men, do not get professional identities nor rise to positions of power without first being educated. In the past, higher education was the prerogative of the male. Not any more. Globally, females are outperforming males in education from kindergarten through to PhD level. In the West, and increasingly in the North, South and East, more women go to university than men, they also get higher grades, and are less likely to drop out. This process of female educational advancement begins in kindergarten and continues through schooling. A 2002 study by the US National Academy of Sciences concluded that boys were "overrepresented in programs for learning disabilities, mental retardation and emotional disturbance, and under-presented in gifted programs". To emphasise this point, New York City's school system recently noted that while 51% of the student body is male, the majority of the student body qualified as gifted is female.

In Europe a recent OECD report, Higher Education to 2030, predicted that women are set to become an even bigger majority of the graduate talent worldwide. In 2005, OECD countries awarded 57% of their degrees to women. This is will go up to over 60% over the next decade. In Sweden, one of the countries ahead of the trend, within 10 years eight out of ten graduates will be women. Even in the Middle East we are seeing dramatic changes; in Qatar 746 women enter university for every 100 men, 247 women for every 100 men in Kuwait, 178 for every 100 men in the UAE, and 120 women for every 100 men in Saudi Arabia.

It is no surprise then, that some international companies, such as Shell, are having to ensure they don't swing their graduate hiring too far in favour of women; but inevitably they, and companies like them, will have little choice - the pool of high quality graduate talent in the near future will be overwhelming female, not male.

As you can see, we are only at the beginnings of this profound gender shift, but for sure women are not going back in their

20th century gender box. The implications for male-female relationships are profound.

Educate women and you immediately trigger the rapid process of social change that leads inexorably to the changes in attitudes towards sex and relationships that we are seeing around the world today. There is no avoiding it. And it is no good 'blaming' this gender shift on feminism, as one British cabinet minister recently did. That is just 'Neanderthal' thinking; it has totally failed to see the bigger picture.

Education leads to enhanced employment opportunities, which in turn leads to increased financial security, which then leads to choices having to be made - choices about relationships, marriage, children, divorce, career, where to live and where to work. This is a global change, no longer confined to the West. And it is a change that has come about in just a few decades.

Which leads us to the next big question - how are men responding?

We limit our children's possibilities by telling them they are male or female. We should allow them to find out for themselves

Changing Men

Here are three questions for you:

1. What does it mean to be a man?

2. Can you think of a man who exemplifies masculinity?

3. What do all men have in common?

None of these questions is easily answered. For example, what it means to be a man depends on the familial, cultural and social setting that a male child is born into. A black male teenager growing up in a Johannesburg slum is picking up very different messages about manhood than a white male teenager growing up in a wealthy suburb of Ottawa.

Exemplars of masculinity are usually of no more substance than media imagery; back in the 1950s it might have been John Wayne or Charlton Heston. But which male film star exemplifies masculinity today? There isn't one.

And what about commonalities amongst men? Well, there aren't any. You might argue that all men have penises, but then if a man loses his penis through, say, an accident, does he stop being a man? No. Is a man with a six-inch penis more of a man than one with a three-inch penis? No. Is a six-foot tall man with a six-pack stomach more manly than an obese four-foot tall one? No, or only if you think so but then your viewpoint doesn't make it universally true.

Becoming a man is a process of learning what 'being a man' means in a particular social location. And masculinity is merely the term we give to various male performances; it too is totally socially specific.

Being a man is a process of social presentation - learning a performance that corresponds with the prevailing social notions about men and masculinity. In most countries it means presenting yourself as straight, not gay. In Scotland it is signified by wearing a kilt and blowing bagpipes, while in Tennessee it suggests a cowboy hat and playing the banjo. Manhood for the Hassidic Jewish male requires him to wear a long black overcoat, beard and top hat. The Sikh man will likely wear a turban and carry a kirpan (ceremonial knife). While the British male politician has to wear a dark suit, white shirt and tie whenever in public in order to appear credible, serious and masculine. And age is also a big variable; an adult male at 66 will be giving off a rather different male presentation than he did at 26. For many centuries in Europe a powerful man was expected to wear a long flowing wig and make-up. Today, on the streets of many cities, he could well have a skinhead haircut and tattoos. You want to see a type of masculinity in action? Watch the Sopranos television series. In this you'll see a succession of strange, dysfunctional, adult men, none of which appears to fit into the 21st century, but who somehow exerts power in spite of that.

For millions of males, manhood is just an extension of the playground - only with more serious consequences

When we research men and masculinities we are actually researching the meanings attached to men and how people, of all sexes, respond to them. There are multiple masculinities, countless ways of being a man, and it all changes over time. None of it is predictable and it is certainly not fixed.

That said, there are powerful and persuasive pressures on males to conform to a dominant code of masculinity, aka the Sopranos example. So it takes a strong man to come out and say he is gay if he lives in a society where homosexuality is taboo. It takes a lot of self-belief for a young black man living in East Baltimore to focus on getting into college rather than into the prevailing gang culture. And it is a very centred 21 year old British male who spends his time reading, is teetotal, celibate and not into sport.

Masculinity has always corresponded with what society presumed to be and identified as, 'manliness'. In the past, such male identities might have been quite limited and specific; the reason being that societies tended to be isolated and self-sufficient, consequently the gender codes got reinforced, not challenged. Nowadays we are exposed to so many different ways of being a man that it is impossible to overlay a single definition. Men can be, and are, nurses, secretaries, maids, midwives, kindergarten teachers, beauticians, and househusbands. And if you assume that such men must be effeminate and gay, well that is you thinking in stereotype, not recognising the reality.

Just as there are many ways of being a man, so there are different ways that men are responding to the dramatic changes in gender relationships that I have outlined above.

In the main, I am referring here to straight men, because it is the straight man that invariably has the most difficulty dealing with the changes taking place in modern femininity and womanhood. That is because gay men have to live their lives always in tension with and relation to, what sociologists Professor Adrienne Rich and Professor Raewyn Connell term 'compulsory heterosexuality' and 'hegemonic masculinity'. These are the powerful but simplistic gender codes applied to all males in most countries. Of course, no men easily fit within these plastic masculine models, for the simple reason that they are not natural but enforced through social sanction. Nevertheless, they are not easy for straight men to reject, and in fact many straight men can carry on through their lives imagining them as the real way for a man to behave; so ''real men' get assumed as being straight, physically strong or assertive, sexually active, controlling of their emotions, confident, competitive, and definitely avoiding any action which might suggest they are in any way effeminate. By contrast, by the time they 'come out' most gay men will have had come to terms with these issues and overcome them on a personal level.

Below I identify the three primary responses from men to the changes we are now seeing in modern femininity and in relationships. I label the three different male types 'acceptors', 'resisters', and 'confused'.

Gender power operates like a pair of scales: for women to gain it, men have to lose it

A. The ACCEPTOR

Over past few decades, one of the most interesting changes in straight men and their masculine performance has been the emergence of those who express a significant degree of femininity. In the West they have been termed 'metrosexuals', in the Far East and Southeast Asia they are called 'herbivores' or 'grass-eaters'.

These men are not all the same in their gender performance but they do have some commonalities: they are very comfortable with women taking on a more assertive and powerful role in society; they see women as equals and feel no insecurity or threat to their masculinity by doing so; they will be more willing to accept their share of the household and childcare work and many go on to become full-time househusbands; they do not consider men superior to women but as partners; they are able to express their feelings without recourse to anger or violence and have a high degree of emotional intelligence; they invariably put a lot of effort into their personal hygiene, dress, and overall appearance; they are often into spiritual awareness and generally ensuring their mental and physical well-being; they are invariably educated to university level.

There are different types of men within this group: We have the pro-feminist men, those who strongly support women's rights and have been active in that respect for many years. Examples would be British academics such as Jeff Hearn and David Morgan; Americans such as Michael Messner and Michael Kimmel, and Australians such as Bob Connell and Alan Peterson. Next come the metrosexuals; highly visible examples include David Beckham, Brad Pitt, George Clooney, Bono,

Bill Clinton, Jude Law, Barack Obama, Orlando Bloom, Nick Clegg and Johnny Depp. The metrosexuals are the largest group amongst what I term the 'accepters' and there are many millions of them now, of all ages, around the world. These males have grown up with feminism and women's emergence into power in society and see it as totally normal. In fact, they welcome it. For them, gender equality is a given.

Only when a woman stops looking for the perfect man will she find him

Finally, at the more extreme end of this spectrum, are the Southeast Asian 'herbivores' and 'grass-eaters', so-called because they are totally opposite in presentation and lifestyle to the traditional Asian carnivore males; e.g. the stoical, fierce, emotionally dysfunctional salarymen of South Korea and Japan especially. The herbivore males are having an enormous social impact across East Asia and one can now find them in Thailand, Malaysia, Indonesia, Hong Kong and Singapore. These men are straight, but expressing a very clear femininity; in their hair style and dress code, in the way they conduct their relationships, express their sexuality, and pursue their careers, so much so that they have been termed 'metrosexuals without the testosterone'. Prominent examples include the South Korean footballer, Ahn Jung-Hwan; the South Korean pop star, Rain; and the Japanese actor, Tsuyoshi Kusanagi. This group appears to be growing both in number and cultural influence. A 2009 survey by a Japanese dating agency found that 61% of unmarried men in their 30s identified themselves as herbivores, while a South Korean media consulting company estimates that between 60-70% of men in their early 20s have adopted herbivore or grass-eater lifestyles, especially in their relationships.

These male 'acceptors' signal the biggest change in masculinity for the past 100 years and their cultural and social influence is spreading around the world. To be sure, they come in various guises with some expressing a much more overt femininity than others, nevertheless these men are straight, not gay. Importantly, they are men who, in different ways, have come to accept who women are today and who women aspire to be.

For women seeking relationships with men, the 'acceptors' are a very attractive proposition. These men, especially the metrosexuals, make good lovers as well as good friends; they have the emotional intelligence of gay men, and the sexual desires of straights. They support gender, racial and sexual equality and are into caring about their appearance and health. Many may be narcissistic in their behaviour, especially the herbivore males, but this merely reinforces the fact that they are comfortable with themselves and with exhibiting a more feminine type of masculinity.

However, don't assume that these men are all necessarily going to be faithful in a relationship or indeed monogamous. That depends on the individual man and the type of relationship that he feels he is in. Also, the very fact that they are so in touch with their inner femininity and can express themselves this way without feeling insecure in their masculine identity only makes them more attractive to other women.

Example:

Robin is a 34 year old British male. He lives in London. After leaving school, Robin went to dance academy and, since the age of 22, has been a professional dancer, touring around the world with some of the very best modern dance companies. He has recently begun choreographing dance performances for other companies and has already won awards for this. He is also taking a part-time degree in physiotherapy, in preparation for when he needs a new careear because he is too old to sustain the high physical impact dancing has on his body. Robin has had many relationships since his teens and gets on very well with women of all ages, and with gay men, of whom there are many in the dance profession. Robin married Cathy five years ago. Cathy is 38, a theatre director and also at the top of her profession. They have two children, aged four and six months. Robin and Cathy share much of the childcare load and one of the reasons for him pursuing the physiotherapy qualification is so he can spend more time with his family after qualifying. Robin encapsulates all the characteristics of the modern metrosexual male. He is fit, looks after his body and his health, is educated, career orientated but also very willing to share all aspects of family life with his partner. He has a high degree of emotional intelligence and this also comes across in his dancing, which has a mix of both the feminine and the masculine within it.

B. The RESISTER

> **Macho masculinity is a combustible mix of insecurity, bravado and anger; not only a lack of understanding of femininity, but a deep-rooted fear of it**

This group of men, the 'resisters', occupy the other end of the masculinity spectrum, a world away from the 'acceptors'. The resisters are similar in one respect however, and that is there are different types of men within this group. The most extreme are those I term the 'radical resisters'; these are mostly to be found within particular religions, especially Islam and Christianity, though even Buddhism has a few of these men. They are men who openly and actively resist women's emancipation even down to denying them education, social and personal freedom, political power, any sort of sexual or relationship choice, career opportunities, indeed treating women as they were typically treated centuries ago. This type of masculinity is embedded in a medieval mindset which is highly patriarchal and which assumes men to be the superior gender. Such thinking invariably draws on religious ideology to 'justify' itself. Clearly, radical resisters to gender equality are not new, it is safe to assume they have always been around. However, in a world where most men are not resisters and certainly not radical about it, this type of male increasingly looks like an anachronism; desperately out of touch with modern views of gender and sexuality. At the same time, the increasing sense of isolation that these men will feel, confronted as they are with the pluralism of the 21st century, motivates them to respond in even more radical ways and therefore potentially become more dangerous. Radical resisters tend to hate women, and at the same time, fear them. They are invariably homophobic, prone to violence and extreme emotional responses, and convinced they are right. Their view of women as either whores or Madonnas goes back at least two thousand years and they are doing everything in their power to make sure it lasts another two thousand.

After the 'radicals' come the reactionary conservatives. Typically, these are men who would feel 'women's lib has gone too far' and that men are now the one's who are isolated and marginalised. They tend to see gender as a battle between the sexes and fear that women have gained the upper hand - they don't like this one iota. They may or may not be associated with any particular religion, but they are certainly not liberal minded. The reactionary conservative can be found in all cultures, all ages, and all social groups. They can be highly educated and wealthy, or poor and lowly. What conservative resisters fear most is change. They are nostalgic for an era when the male breadwinner nuclear family was the dominant social model; when women stayed home and raised the family and men went out to work and brought in the money. This will likely be the family type they were raised in and they see no reason to change it. They are against single parent families, sexual freedoms - especially women's - and are usually homophobic. Their view of the world draws a lot on simplistic biological assumptions and Darwinism; that is, they see women and men as inherently different and therefore suited to different, but complementary, roles in society. So the conservative resister would not be promoting equal opportunities, either at work or in the home. In fact, he really believes that gender equality is fundamentally unnatural. He would assume men make the best leaders and managers, and that women are designed only for caring roles, especially nurturing and raising children. This type of man will hate 'political correctness' in all its forms and blow a fuse at the very thought of same-sex marriages. Similarly, he just cannot get his head round the idea of men as nurses, or women as soldiers. Some of these men will be open about their resistance to women's progress others will just stay silent and fume from the sidelines at most aspects of 21st century society.

Finally, we have the emotional distancers. These are men who have, through their personal experiences of typically, divorce, child-maintenance, unemployment or simply 'bad relationships' come to fear modern woman. In his mind, she has taken his job and left him bereft of employment; been totally unreasonable in a divorce settlement and left him near bankruptcy and without fair access to his children; or she has hurt him so badly in the past that he cannot bring himself to get into another relationship again. He never started out hating women, but this is where his mindset takes him at times. He certainly doesn't understand women nor empathise with them. He would deny it of course, but the reality is there are times when he wants revenge. Like all the resisters, the emotional distancer is carrying a lot of anger, underpinned by anxiety and deep insecurity about his manhood, and his future. He is drawn to women, but never fully trusts them. Maybe he did have a genuinely bad experience in the past, but this type of man lacks the emotional reflexivity to see that this was just one woman and not representative of the whole female species. Some of these men can harbour grudges and fear of women from as far back as their teens, when they might have experienced a painful rejection from some young woman. However, of all three main types of resister, this man has the most chance of changing. He can be nurtured and coaxed out of his shell and brought into the light of modern living. He is a vulnerable male, lacking confidence around women; a man who, for many reasons, was always going to be very emotionally exposed in love from the outset. But if he meets a woman who truly loves and understands him, and is patient while his fears and angers subside, he will bloom again.

All these resisters are vulnerable to ideologies that purport to tell them they are 'special' and that it is society that needs changing. So one can find them in any male-dominated group that has such ideas at its core; not only religious but also nationalistic and racist (e.g. 'white supremacy'). Extreme-minded members can be very prone to violence. Other commonalities amongst the resister type men are a desire for control of women; fear of lack of control in their lives generally; deep insecurity around women who are assertive and independent; anxiety about their manhood and masculine identity; general angst about modern society; emotional immaturity; social isolation; lack of reflexivity; poor empathy with others; and a barely submerged anger which can quickly surface in disagreements with those closest to them and whom they purport to love the most. Many of these men are hurting and if they are pushed or feel isolated too much then they have the capacity to hurt back.

Example:

Mark is a 33 year old Australian. His main home is in Sydney, but because of his work he travels the world. Mark is an international celebrity; an actor. He is wealthy, successful and with many fans. Mark can play most any film role, and has done. But he is especially convincing in the 'hard man' type role. These roles have made him famous. In terms of his private life, Mark has experienced less

*success. It is not that he has had so many relationships, he hasn't;
well, no more than any other man would have in his situation.
No, Mark's problem is his attitude towards women. Mostly, Mark
is paternalistic if not patronising. He prefers to be in control in
his relationships and if he feels that slipping away he can get very
emotional. At worst he responds violently in arguments. This violent
element to his personality began in childhood when he witnessed his
father's misogynistic attitude and violence towards his mother, and
has continued since. Women are drawn to his testosterone-fuelled
masculine performance, but emotionally Mark is vulnerable and
insecure. It is this edgy and nervous contradiction that is the essence
of his acting ability, but when it constantly surfaces in his most
intimate relationships then it becomes a major problem. Two years
ago, after several appearances in court over domestic abuse charges
and a long-time girlfriend leaving him for the last time, Mark
sought help. Now he regularly attends a self-help group for men who
are violent towards women they love. He now recognises where his
anger comes from and is trying hard to change.*

C. The CONFUSED

Being confused isn't as big a problem as not realising it

Experiencing a sense of confusion and bafflement at the modern
world is not unreasonable - most of us do at some point. There
is so much happening around us, to us, a growing recognition
of the chaos and unpredictability of life, that it becomes almost
impossible to hold on to some larger perspective and see the
bigger picture. The big picture just keeps on getting bigger and
more confusing, which in turn makes us feel so much smaller. It
is like living in an urban metropolis inhabited by millions and
dominated by massive skyscrapers. Every day there are more
people, more buildings, a changing landscape that no one appears
in total control of, and within this we have to find ourselves, be

ourselves. Not easy. We just feel tiny and insignificant; insecure and disconnected, even while living alongside millions of other such disconnected souls.

Maybe it was always like this. After all, if you were a European youth in 1914 then you were about to live (if you survived) through two world wars, a global influenza pandemic, several European civil wars and revolutions, the Cold War, the Cuba Crisis, and a technological and knowledge transformation like no other before it. But at least you had a fairly constant sense of masculinity to hold on to. Back in 1914, men went off to fight and women stayed home and nursed the injured, and when the soldier recovered and the fighting over, he was sure to get work in a factory making something and if he was middle class then he could expect to step into the office or boardroom. The world was at least predictable for men in that respect.

The confused male of the 21st century has little that is predictable around him. He has a lot to handle and one of the most troubling issues is just being a man; he has to try and understand what women want and also what he wants. The male signposts have all got turned around or have just disappeared altogether. The rules of gender have been thrown out the window. Sometimes it seems to him that women still want a tough, strong guy, and yet when he acts like this in a relationship it causes him all sorts of problems. So he tries being quiet and more withdrawn but then gets accused of being 'out of touch with his emotions'. He always assumed that women were attracted to men with power and money, and he can see plenty of evidence that they still are. Yet most of the women he knows earn as much as he does, live single lives quite independently of any man, and are doing very nicely thank you.

The sex act is, however, still to his advantage. He does have something many women want. One of the changes he senses in women is their heightened sexual desire, or at least their heightened expectations of sexual satisfaction. He likes sex and lots of it, and so do the women he has relationships with. However, while he would never admit it to anyone, this does sometimes feels like pressure. Occasionally he feels a little objectified, used. It is almost as if he is under notice to provide satisfaction or else. This can be a real sexual turn-off.

It is not that he doesn't like and respect women, he does. The problem is Mr Confused just feels out of his depth with modern woman. Many of his male friends are the same. They are single or divorced; in and out of relationships, most of which don't last more than a few months. He also sees more men, including friends of his, still living with their parents, still being looked after by mum even in their 30s. He puts this down to the cost of housing, but when he looks around him he doesn't see so many women in their 30s still living with mum and dad. They have their own homes.

But at least he has sport. This is one area of Mr Confused life that is still very much about men and their masculinity. Every Saturday afternoon he either goes to the football match to support his team or watches it on tv with his mates. This ritual celebration of manhood lasts all of 90 minutes but it has become a constant theme in his life. It is one area where he feels good about himself, which he can relate to and talk about with masculine confidence.

There are, of course, other distractions. He has his male friends and they go off to the bar regularly, or even occasionally to some suntrap in Europe or Asia for ten days, where the girls are very willing, and not too expensive. And then there is the computer - always available to spice up his life through porn, virtual worlds, or on-line dating.

Mr Confused is actually discovering how to retreat in the face of modern gender reality. Men just like him, around the world, are retreating to sport, computer games, sex tourism, or just work. They are not inclined to marriage - indeed not many women they meet are up for marriage anyway - and as far as kids are concerned they couldn't afford them. Living with mum and dad is a big attraction for obvious reasons. Though there will come a time when mum and dad are not around.

Occasionally, Mr Confused meets a woman who really attracts him and he goes all out to try and be the sort of man he thinks she wants him to be. He listens to her, tries to share his feelings, act not too traditionally, be very attentive in bed, and avoid talking too much about sport and cars. But it is hard work and he ends up wondering whether it is actually worth the effort. Even more disconcerting, he senses there may be other men in her life. She is the one who usually decides when they will meet and she clearly likes her own space. He would like to see her every weekend, but she won't agree. Seems she has a full social life without him. Actually, she has more friends than he has.

Then there is another type of confused man - one who doesn't know he is, but suddenly finds out. This type is usually older, lived a traditional married life for many years, and from this cosy and predictable setting watched the world go by. He has probably absorbed himself in being a good husband and provider and never felt confused at all about his masculinity. But then something changes. It could be illness, the trauma of death in the family, redundancy, impotence, retirement, his wife going off with another man, his children growing up gay or just different to what he'd hoped. Whatever it is, this traumatic incident forces him to reappraise his life and when he does he realises very quickly that world is not how he thought it was. It is not just different it is chaotic. Again, all the longstanding masculine cues are overturned, disrupted. Why has he failed? What sort of man is he? What sort of man do his friends and family think he is? All very troubling, all very profound; some men can move on from this to becoming acceptors, some men will retreat, some men will get angry. Many will get depressed or go into a state of denial.

The evidence for men retreating in the face of 21st century life pressures is quite persuasive. Japan has the hikikomori; perhaps one million males aged from 13 - 25 years old who have literally shut themselves off from the outside world, typically spending 23 hours a day in their bedrooms - watching movies, surfing the Internet, totally isolated. They are now starting to emerge in Taiwan and South Korea. A 2009 UK national survey revealed that a third of men under 40 are still living at 'Hotel Mum', and are twice as likely to be doing so than women. Across the West, men's health experts are reporting dramatic increases in the number of men aged 18-30 who are using Viagra and reporting erectile dysfunctionality. Relationship counsellors put this down to the 'Sex in the City' phenomena; leaving many men feeling emasculated by modern women.

Social isolation, inability to handle modern relationships, anxiety over sexual performance, the ubiquitous threat of unemployment, plus heightened work and financial pressures all combine to create real confusion and stress for many men today. The old assumptions about men's role in society have gone, and nothing has replaced them. Women are ambitious, confident, and assertive. A recent survey suggested that 88% of British women expect equality in a relationship and less than 20% are attracted to men who adopt a traditional role. When women don't find partners who are non-traditional, then they settle for being single. And increasingly they are doing so.

One really disturbing outcome of modern man's confusion is depression. And it is getting much worse. It is a myth that women are more prone to depression than men; they are just better at getting it treated. Men, by contrast, tend to suffer in silence fearful of appearing weak or insecure. Men suffering from depression can become animated, aggressive and angry. They can turn to drink and drugs. And they can turn to suicide. The highest suicide risk group in the UK is now men aged between 40 and 49. Three quarters of all suicides are male. In the last 45 years suicide rates have increased by 60% worldwide with males four times more likely to die of suicide than females. And young men especially are experiencing depression and committing suicide. Suicide rates amongst young males have been increasing to such an extent that they are now the group at highest risk in a third of all countries.

Example:

Barry is a 29 year-old male, living in the town of Huntsville, Ontario. He is single and lives with his retired parents, both of whom are aged 64. Barry has an older sister, Mary, but she went off to university in Toronto when she was 18 and is now working in Vancouver. Barry always found school boring so when he had the opportunity to leave and get a job as a car mechanic at a local garage, he took it. He has been working in the same garage for 12 years now and sees no other future. He doesn't earn that much but his living costs are low and he is able to enjoy nights out with his mates and occasionally take a trip into Toronto. Some weekends he goes camping in the nearby national parks. Barry first had sex at age 16, but has had few girlfriends since, and nothing really serious. There was one special girlfriend a few years back, but like many women her age she too left the small town of Huntsville to work in Toronto. Barry's big love is sport - in the winter he follows hockey, in the summer, lacrosse. Some weekends he goes to see the matches live, otherwise he watches on television. If he is not down at the local bar in an evening, Barry spends time on his computer. He has joined two on-line dating agencies and is in regular email communication with a few women, mostly living in Canada. However, the cost of travel makes it difficult for him to actually meet them. He watches a lot of Internet porn, and while it gives him with some satisfaction, he sometimes feels he spends too much time watching the stuff. He would consider himself easy-going but doesn't find it easy to talk about himself nor to talk to women. Barry considers himself a 'man's man' and is hoping that one day a woman will come along who appreciates what that means.

The hardest performance for any man is learning how to convincingly be one

Chapter 3: Understanding Love

"We love to know that we are not alone" (C.S.Lewis)

'Love', the most cliché ridden, overused and abused word in the English language - and the most powerful. We use the word to attract, to deceive, to motivate, to control. We can use the word glibly but at the same time convey the most profound meaning. You might say 'I love you' out of pity, out of guilt, and sometimes when you truly mean it. Love speaks across a thousand languages and is in every culture; it has sustained art, music and literature for millennia. Love has caused wars, slaughtered millions in its name and created oceans of grief yet still we yearn for it.

No book on relationships could be written without using the word 'love', and this book is no exception. You, the reader, are hoping for some new insight, perhaps a revelation, or at least a confirmation, about love. Which is entirely reasonable, because almost certainly 'love' will have touched your life, perhaps even deep soulmate love. However, I am equally sure this experience left you feeling, at different times, vulnerable as well as reassured, anxious as well as confident, ecstatic as well as miserable. Perhaps you are still in this 'love moment', or maybe you seek it once more? Equally, you may never want to go there again.

Yet despite the risks that 'being in love' brings, who would wish to go to a fortune-teller only to be told "you will never have love in your life"? Would that not be the most damaging, hurtful and wretched state to be in - to know, or imagine, that you will never experience or receive love?

For the vast majority of us, not experiencing love is not the problem. The problem is handling love when it arrives and dealing with the aftermath when it has gone. We all need guidelines, and this chapter provides some.

Two hundred thousand years of human love, and still it remains a mystery

Falling

The phrase 'falling in love' is so apt. The experience is akin to falling - being very aware you will hit the ground at some point, but not sure when. And certainly not sure what state you'll be in afterwards. Some of us may be floating downwards on a cloud, others are plunging headfirst; it is exciting and it is addictive. The feeling of being in love triggers hormonal responses in us that are not dissimilar to the chemical highs we can get from certain drugs. Which is why there are growing numbers of counsellors treating 'love addiction'. There are those who just cannot cope without their regular 'love fix'.

What triggers a love attraction between two people is impossible to predict, package, categorise or clarify. It can be anything; appearance, voice, smell, image, a touch, a few words, plus a whole host of other factors not least of which is what is going on in the head of the individual at the time. The person who attracts us at 21 is unlikely to attract us in quite the same way when we are 51. Similarly, we can fall in love with someone in our 30s marry them, but a decade later wonder why. Indeed, such 'love reappraisals' can happen in just a week or so and often do.

I am 62 and I have felt myself in love with at least ten different women since the age of 20. Yet would any of those women attract me today; only my current love. I am equally sure my past loves would say the same about me.

We can never fully understand the loves of others. Nor they of ours

If I try and look back to the sort of man I was during each of those past ten loves, then I have a real difficulty recognising him. He is a stranger. I know it was 'me' but who 'me' was in 1970, 1980, 1990, even 2000, I am not so sure. The past is indeed another country, and its one invested with a lot of myth and delusion. This is especially so about love. It is just too easy to be nostalgic about ended love relationships; viewing past love through the blue mists of memory is a powerful seduction in itself. Nostalgia is probably healthy, but so too is a good dose of realism, especially when it comes to love relationships.

If we are going to be realistic about love then we have to start with recognising one core truth to love - basically it is an illusion. That is, it is not real in the way a mountain or river is real. Love is an emotion and emotions are highly fluid and very unreliable, especially over the long term. At the same time, the pain that we can feel from romantic rejection, lost love, is as sharp as any knife. Recent research shows that love pain is akin to physical pain - our brains don't distinguish. So next time someone tells you they are 'hurting from love', you can take it literally.

We have this powerful emotion within us but its unreliable; much as we would like to, we cannot fully trust love. This is not to say that a feeling of love cannot last, it can. But it cannot last without changing. All feelings of love change, though it doesn't automatically follow that we should end a relationship as a result. Some loves grow slow but strongly and from fairly inauspicious beginnings, while other loves flame up quickly but die out just as dramatically. All loves have high and low points. Again, recognising what type of love we have, or want, is an important first step to understanding love.

There is another aspect to love which we prefer not to think about but which is ever-present; the functional aspect. Despite love being an overwhelming emotion, it is not so overwhelming that we don't apply some rational thinking to it. You may imagine you fell in love in an instant, perhaps 'across a crowded room'. Maybe, but even in that moment your brain did some lightening calculations, and its been doing them ever since. Obviously you assessed sex and gender, but you also assessed age, facial expressions, height, size, dress, body language. And that was just in the first sixty seconds and across a crowded room, or maybe a noisy nightclub dance-floor.

Don't feel bad, when it comes to falling in love we all tick boxes.

In this chapter I am going to describe the three main types of romantic love.

- Wishful Love

- Consensus Love

- Soulmate Love

I am not concerned with other aspects of love, e.g. for family, friends, pets, objects. I am solely interested in understanding love as it emerges in sexual relationships. Finally, its important to recognise that everything I discuss in terms of love is equally applicable for same-sex relationships as it is for hetero relationships.

Delusion is the food of love - reality starves it

Wishful Love

Do you recall the first time you 'fell in love'? You were in your teens, still at school or college, and life was a combustible mix of adolescent angst, sexual desire, insecurity, and boundless hope for the future. You were supposed to be studying, but actually most of your waking time was taken up with thinking about the opposite (or same) sex. You were masturbating several times a day and if you weren't pleasuring yourself then someone else was. And all the while you were trying so hard to be cool, mature, one of the gang, confident - accepted. You were nervously discovering who you could be; a process that was both thrilling and terrifying at the same time.

Yes, heady days. And in amongst all this emotional noise arrives that special someone, the individual who somehow manages to encapsulate your dreams of perfect love and togetherness. You occasionally allow yourself to imagine a future with them, living in a house on the hill, maybe with two delightful, healthy, happy children. Sometimes this desire feels so desperate you ache from it, other times it slips from your mind altogether.

I could call this 'puppy love' but then that wouldn't do it justice. I could call this 'true love' but again, that would be inappropriate also. What you felt at that time is what I term 'Wishful Love', and the French describe as *l'armour fou* (crazy love). It is love based solely on your imaginings, your hopes, your dreams and desires. What it is not based on is reality. In fact, wishful love cannot handle reality in any form whatsoever. A dose of reality when one is experiencing wishful love has the same effect as an ice cold shower. It wakes you up and fast.

We can all expect to experience wishful love at some point in our life. I have experienced it twice; first in my early teens, then again when I was 51; a gap of nearly four decades but with some revealing parallels.

In both instances I was needy for love. I felt a little alone, emotionally vulnerable and my romantic sensibilities were in overdrive. I was looking for love, though didn't realise it at the time. Inside I was insecure and anxious about what came next in my life; part of me excited by the prospect of change, another part very apprehensive. At the time and in my mind, each of these wishful loves of my life were the key to the future; they would make me content and secure inside, they would walk the future pathway with me; they would remove the fear and uncertainty simply by being present in my life.

Well, that is what I imagined and hoped. As I say, not reality.

The two women were as different as women can be. The first was aged just 16, same age as I; British, pretty, demure, shy, virginal, and in my eyes the most perfect female that ever walked the earth. Whenever I met her socially (we never actually dated) I was just a blushing, hopeless wreck.

My second wishful love was a bar girl I met in Bangkok. She was 33. I was 51 and it was my first time to Thailand. I will call her Joy. Joy had worked in the Thai sex industry for at least 4 years and had a 9 year old daughter by a married Thai businessman. This man had been a long-term boyfriend of Joy when she was in her 20s. Joy's daughter lived with her father, and he made sure Joy rarely saw her. Joy was certainly not virginal, though she was attractive. Joy's background and work did not bother me, I loved her: so much so that I wanted to pay for her to learn English, quit her night job, and start a new life with me in the UK. I even explored the possibility of her studying at a British university. All crazy of course, but at the time it seemed to me entirely reasonable and, if I was determined enough, possible to make happen.

In total, I spent no more than 14 days and nights in Thailand with this second wishful love. And for much of that time we argued. Not an auspicious beginning. But Joy seemed to care for me in a way that no woman had ever cared for me before, and she needed me. I wanted to protect her, to make her happy.

The power of that wishful love was immense and it sustained me for many months, long after the last time I saw Joy, which was seeing her standing forlorn and sad, waving me off one night at Bangkok airport. I kept in contact with Joy for several months afterwards and made plans for a return visit to Thailand. But it never happened. Someone else came into my life and this new love helped me get over Joy, my second wishful love.

Being in love is an ongoing romance with one's imagination

By the time I was 50 I had already been married twice and was living with my third partner. I had four children from three long-term, consecutive, relationships. I had also had the occasional girlfriend. I was experienced. Or so I thought. My first encounter with Thai femininity quickly revealed to me just how inexperienced I really was. That exposure to a very different type of femininity happened to coincide with one of the big relationship shifts in my life, when I was about to split up from my third long-term partner and leave two children. Under the circumstances, and looking back with hindsight, wishful love was inevitable.

Experience won't necessarily make us immune from wishful love; it can strike us all. However, it needs certain emotional conditions to flourish; a feeling of being alone together with profound uncertainty over where your life is heading combine to create a deep-rooted insecurity in your sense of self. Basically, you want someone to hold your hand while you step forward into the next part of your life journey. You imagine that this special someone can resolve these inner dilemmas. It is all about you, not them.

As I say, wishful love feeds off need; specifically, vast, subconscious emotional insecurity.

Wishful love emerges in our minds through displacement and projection. That is, we are displacing our emotional needs onto the other. We then project all our hopes for the future onto this person who, in our minds, now has the capacity to resolve our inner dilemmas. The fact that we invariably know very little about our love object, who they really are, matters little, in fact it helps to be ignorant of that reality. In our minds, the mental portrait we have created of them is the 'reality' and this we will hang on to for as long as possible.

I know all love has an element of this, but with wishful love it is the central characteristic; it is the single element that sustains the feeling of love and does this despite the utter irrationality of it all. We are actually falling in love not with another person, but with the dream of what that person can bring us. Our minds conjure up a romantic scenario; we then invest so much emotional energy and hope in this dream that it becomes extremely difficult to face the fact that it is only an illusion.

Let me give you another typical example of how this happens in the 21st century.

Julie

Julie is a 49 year old British woman. She is a headteacher; a middle class, educated professional. Julie is divorced, has two grown up children, and lives alone just outside London. She is mature, experienced in relationships and appears confident, especially in her work. Julie has had several boyfriends since her divorce, 10 years ago, including one man with whom she lived for four years. She is currently dating a man she met on the Internet. Julie first started using online dating two years after her divorce. For her, it was a simple and private way of meeting suitable partners. Her divorce had shaken her up emotionally and at times she felt depressed and lonely. Work pressures were multiplying and her confidence in herself as an attractive, sexual person was ebbing away. Julie had not experienced love from a man for many years and she now yearned for a loving, romantic encounter. The first man she really connected with online was Bob. She and Bob began emailing each and by the end of the first week had exchanged over 100 emails. By the end of third week they had exchanged over 400. The email exchanges quickly went from friendly, to intimate, to sexual. She told Bob she loved him sometime into the second week, and Bob responded likewise. For Julie, it was one of the most intensely romantic experiences of her life. She felt a love for Bob that she had never felt for her ex-husband. This feeling of love continued for a further two weeks, right up until she and Bob actually met. They continued the relationship in real time for a further month and then Julie finished it. Only after actually starting a full relationship with Bob did Julie awake to the fact that he was not the man she had imagined him to be.

Email is a particularly powerful medium for conveying love feelings. Indeed, all aspects of Internet social networking carry the same emotional risks; especially for those of us who are going through a difficult time and feeling needy and insecure. Like Julie, we project our yearnings and dreams onto the other person, often without having actually met them and certainly without knowing them as individuals. The other person unwittingly and unknowingly becomes the receptacle into which we place all our hopes. And because email is so instant, so immediate in its exchange, so the feeling of love emerges rapidly. In Julie's case, it took just over a week for full-blown wishful love to kick in. And when it did, it was overwhelming.

Julie's experience is very common. Words conjure up images, and the images stick in our head. We can read so much into a simple exchange of words, even emails - if we want to. As I have stressed, wishful love is not based on reality but on hope. This whole process carries many risks. It is dangerous because it is not based on rational and insightful understanding of the other person - it is based entirely on an identity that we have conjured up in our minds. We then hang on to it fearful of letting go for to let go will plunge us back into the realms of loneliness and isolation; we are dreading the thought of never finding such love again. Julie was strong enough to realise what had happened and broke off her relationship with Bob. Many of us, men and women, are not so strong and instead we carry on in hope, failing to confront and accept the reality of it all.

Wishful love is based on illusion and while all love has some aspect of illusion attached to it, wishful love is entirely illusionary. There is nothing real behind it; it is sustained only by the imaginary identity we have created of the person 'we love'.

So is wishful love only ever negative? No. Like all loves, wishful love does have some positives.

To understand the positives we need to go back to the reason why wishful love came into our life in the first place, which was largely because of our emotional needs at a particular time; our acute feelings of emptiness and our deep uncertainty about the future.

Wishful love can be the means by which we move on from that state of distress and anxiety into a new place of hope, self-confidence and self-awareness. It can provide us with the courage to face the future and the confidence to meet new lovers. It can be the means by which we move from a feeling of isolation into socialisation and interaction. And it can provide us with a lot of self-knowledge. But this will only happen after we have let it go. The learning begins once we accept the reality of it all, have reflected on what is going on with us and with our love object, recognise that this is wishful love and then release ourselves from it. While we are in it we are too caught up in the emotional noise to reflect on the bigger picture. Yes, the experience of such a powerful emotional moment will touch us deeply and while aspects of it might be very painful ultimately we can learn from it all. It can make us stronger, more reflexive and thereby improve our self-esteem. After all, it is love and while wishful love is never going to be the same as a soulmate relationship, just experiencing the emotional rush can make us feel positive about ourselves, our capacity to attract others, our sense of the future.

Never regret having experienced wishful love - just see it as one item in the love repertoire available to you. But this only works so long as you learn from the experience. The risk is in not wanting to let it go. This is a highly dangerous response, especially if you are already in a relationship that is largely positive but maybe lacks that spark of sex and romance. Wishful love cannot replace a long-term love relationship and ultimately it cannot bring you contentment. However, by providing you with a strong sense of having someone in your life who 'loves you', wishful love can give you the strength and confidence necessary to leave a relationship that has come to the end of its time. Just don't imagine that wishful love will ever be the big love of our life.

Illusory Aspect: Very High

Practical Aspect: Very Low

Emotive Aspect: High

Long-Term Prospect: Very Low

Consensus Love

As I indicate above, all love relationships have some functional element to them, whether it is fulfilling an emotional need in us, or meeting some material expectation. In the early stages of a love relationship these sorts of reflections and assessments are particularly important. How we answer them can indicate just where the love comes from and where it is going. And we cannot answer them unless we know the other person very well indeed, and they us.

This type of evaluation is fundamental to consensus love; because it is a type of love based on awareness and acceptance of the other party, recognition of who they are and what they want, and is comfortable with their identity. There is little illusion attached to it; the whole process has a strong functional dimension. The initial relationship may well be sparked by sexual attraction, personal and cultural harmony, but then added to this are the material conditions. If the material conditions work for both of you then what emerges is a very powerful understanding, an agreement, a consensus about your future together. How this works is that we are basically asking ourselves what this new love in our life can bring us and do for us, in terms of our overall life journey. Concerns and questions such as:

Children: e.g. Will this person want children?

Money: e.g. Does this person have employment?

Work: e.g. Will this person help me with my work/business?

Family: e.g. What will my family make of the relationship?

Property: e.g. Will I have to sell my home and live with them?

Age: e.g. Is he/she the right age for me?

Status: e.g. Does this person enhance or detract from my social status?

Location: e.g. This person lives in another country: do I want to move?

Relationships: e.g. Am I prepared to leave a current partner for this person?

Lifestyle: e.g. Can I live with this person - do I like their lifestyle?

Religion: e.g. Will this person expect me to convert to their religion?

[The one element that tends not to get considered too critically, at least in the early stages of the love relationship, is the sex element. This is because sex and sexual attraction is likely to be there from the beginning anyway, usually quite powerfully. Without it, there is not going to be a relationship in the first place. However, as I discuss in Chapter 5, for a range of reasons sex often becomes the big issue as time passes.]

I know this all might seem rather selfish, calculative and instrumental, but actually it is entirely normal and quite reasonable. Love is not just an emotional commitment it invariably carries a material one too. If we are intent on this love developing then it is most likely we will end up sharing pretty much every aspect of our life with our lover. In which case, it is entirely reasonable to ask some fairly profound questions first.

And there are two direct questions to ask yourself to determine whether you are in consensus love as opposed to wishful love or soulmate love. Ask yourself why you love someone. You will probably answer by saying you love that person 'for who they are'. Fine, now ask yourself if you can truly accommodate any change whatsoever in that person without it in any way damaging or lessening your love for them. If you can say you would accommodate any change, if there are absolutely no conditions to your love, then you have what I call 'soulmate love' and I describe that type of love below. But if you recognise and accept that there are limits to your love, if you have particular expectations of what you expect from your lover if you are to carry on loving them, being with them, then this indicates you have a much more common type of love - consensus love.

Is 'consensus love', 'true love'? Absolutely, and it is very powerful. In fact, most of us experience this type of love during our lives. From consensus love come medium to long-term relationships - they can last. This type of love is built on strong foundations - where both parties have made an assessment of their future together and find that all aspects fit. The jigsaw is complete and so is their understanding of each other. It is a real working, functioning, partnership.

Don't rely on love. Rely on yourself

Unlike wishful love, consensus love is fully aware of the other person, the love focus; who they are and what they are. It is not based on illusion.

The power of this love is precisely the realisation that we have met someone who 'ticks all our boxes'. There are few if any accommodations to be made - it clearly works on all levels. And on top of that we have the sexual factor sustaining the intimacy, at least in the early stages of the relationship.

Why wouldn't we 'fall in love'?

But consensus love does come with one vital condition. And that one condition is that it must 'work for us'.

If it ever stops working for us then the love goes. As I stress, it is a mutual contract.

Consensus love is especially common in those relationships where there is a lot of balance, for example in couples who are both young or both older, typically aged 50 upwards. This applies in both gay and straight love partnerships. The reason being that younger and older lovers, if they are of a similar age and background, have so much in common to start with that the love develops out of a clear mutuality; emotional and material. Consensus love is more risky when we are in the midst of great changes in our life, perhaps in our 30s or 40s. In these stages of our life journey consensus love is vulnerable to the transformations going on around us.

Here are two vignettes both of which illustrate consensus love:

Marie and Saul

Marie is 27, and studying at Ohio State University medical school. She has a boyfriend, Saul, 28, also studying at the same medical school. They have been together for four years . Marie and Saul live together in rented accommodation not far from the university. Most of their time is taken up with studying, though each also has part-time work. Because they are similar ages, Marie and Saul are expecting to graduate around the same time and then intend to apply for work as junior hospital doctors. They are middle class, educated, and similar in culture and background. They have met each other's families and there is a strong social and well as love bond between them. Their friendship group contains both other students on the programme and friends from their respective hometowns. For Marie and Saul, the immediate future is fairly predictable, thereafter they intend to work as doctors, preferably in a large town, not a city, and once established professionally, get married and have children. They talk a lot about their future together - the sort of house they would like to buy, income, and family life. They have very similar values and ideals. Both are Christian, though not much into religion. They are very much in love.

Lucy and Peter

Lucy is 58. Peter is 65. They are married, retired and live in Toronto. Lucy used to be a government officer. Peter was a Superintendent in the Canadian Mounted Police. Lucy and Peter are grandparents. They each have children from previous marriages. Lucy was married once before, and divorced 15 years ago. Peter has been married twice previously and divorced for 10 ten years. Between them, they have five children and four grandchildren, living in Canada, USA and Hong Kong. Lucy's two children live in Toronto, including her daughter who is married with two children. Lucy and Peter met through an online dating agency and began seeing each other four years ago. They were married last year. They each sold their respective homes and bought a property in a quiet suburb of Toronto. They prefer to be in the city for its cultural life and shopping. On weekends in summer they often drive to one of the national parks for camping, or sail their boat on Lake Ontario. Lucy likes to spend time with her daughter and grandchildren, who she sees most weeks. They have a wide circle of friends, keep fit and enjoy an active social life. They each have good pensions. Their main concern is to stay healthy and to be together for the rest of their lives.

In both these vignettes the consensus love can be seen as based on mutual understanding of how to live in the present, what each couple's respective priorities are, and what the future might hold for them. This future is imagined and different for each couple, but it corresponds strongly with where each person is on their particular life journey. The pieces in the relationship jigsaw fit together nicely. For example, there is a very good likelihood that Marie and Saul will continue their relationship through medical school. However, once they reach the point of applying for jobs then this could be a problem time for them. It is quite possible they will get jobs in different parts of the country, at which point the relationship has dropped its originally consensus and they will split up. Their respective pathways diverge.

Lucy and Peter have both had the 'big loves' of their lives, both actually have had soulmates, partners they loved, lived with for many years and with whom they raised a family. For different reasons, those marriages ended and they found themselves alone. Now they have each other and the bond of love feels as strong as it ever was in their earlier marriages. But it is different. Again, the consensus is based around sustaining a particular lifestyle. Neither Lucy nor Peter could handle a lot of change in their relationship. For example, if one of them wanted to take up a hobby which omitted the other, or move to another part of Canada. They can handle health issues; they are mentally prepared for that. But big lifestyle changes, not.

Consensus love is weak when it comes to self-sacrifice and this is what makes it so different from soulmate love, which I describe below. So long as the consensus is maintained, then so is the love. This in no way diminishes the love feeling; it just signals that it is different and based primarily on a strong functionality and clear expectations of what both parties are bringing to the relationship.

Love is not as spontaneous as we like to think: we all tick boxes before falling

Consensus love has always been around, but it is especially visible today, in an age when we tend to put ourselves first, seek to protect our individuality, material status, and function as independent beings in every respect. We have a powerful desire for love but on our terms; we want to try and minimise the risks if at all possible while protecting what we have. Many consensus loves go so far as to establish a written contract to the relationship, e.g. a prenuptial agreement, and these are becoming more common.

Whether or not it is clarified by some written agreement, consensus love works almost as a defined contract; the couple confirm the dimensions and boundaries to the relationship: This can cover anything and everything, it is up to the couple. For example; agreeing to have and raise children together, and if they cannot have children then adopting; agreeing to separate bank accounts but sharing all expenses; agreeing to be monogamous but if one has sex outside the relationship to tell the other about it; agreeing to share their leisure time together but each take separate holiday once a year; agreeing to live in the city and not the country.

However, life is not predictable. We change, our circumstances and needs change. Consensus love is not very flexible nor very accommodating. It is a love based on awareness of the other person, their character and identity, but as I have said above, identities don't stay fixed throughout our lives.

In the past, most marriages were based on consensus love built around predictable gender roles. The man in the relationship was fulfilled and validated in his role as masculine protector, male breadwinner, provider, patriarch and overall head of the family. The woman in the relationship was fulfilled and validated in her role as feminine nurturer, protector, housewife, matriarch and head of the domestic sphere. Marriages lasted for life on precisely this arrangement and consensus love was their foundation.

Similarly, around the world, we can still see arranged marriages that are entirely based on an instrumental functionality, a predetermined set of expectations and roles that each party is required to adhere to. Any love that emerges from such arranged marriages, as it can over time, will almost certainly be consensus love.

But what of consensus love in an age when the gender roles have disappeared, or even been reversed? What of consensus love in a time of constant and unpredictable transformation? What of consensus love in an era when we place greater emphasis on our needs, our journey? This is the reality of 21st century relationships, an age when increasing numbers of us are in pursuit of self-actualisation, perhaps even prone to narcissism. In these circumstances, love can go almost as fast as it arrives, which is one reason why we are now seeing so many loves floundering.

One way to handle this difficulty is simply to establish a new contract, a new consensus. In this way so the love, and the relationship, can continue. This is something I explore more fully in the final chapter to this book when I describe the Manifesto Rules'.

In the example of Marie and Saul, this 'new contract' might mean them agreeing to put one of their medical careers before the other; for example, whoever gets the best job the other follows. In which case they don't need to split up, they just readjust to the new reality. For Lucy and Peter it could mean that they decide to have holidays apart while Peter goes to visit his children and grandchildren in Hong Kong.

Similarly, I have met couples who have consensus love and have stayed together for many years but only by reinventing their love contract. For some, this might mean allowing one partner to have sex outside the relationship, but no longer having sex together. For others, it might require them to renegotiate time apart, independent of each other.

All relationships go through different phases, mirroring our life's love journey. To keep consensus love going we need to build in more flexibility. The more flexible it is, the more chance it has of lasting.

The strength of consensus love is that both parties get to agree the terms of the relationship; they jointly contribute to the 'contract'. This is calculative, but it does provide an extremely strong foundation upon which to build the relationship. From this beginning, so you go into the future with some sense of security. But as I stress, couples also need to factor in the flexible, 'what if' aspect.

Build in the possibility of change, because for sure change will come.

Illusory Aspect: Very Low

Practical Aspect: Very High

Emotive Aspect: Medium to High

Long-term Prospects: Medium to Very High

Soulmate Love

Soulmates never fully part, they just agree to go their separate ways

One of the most common questions I am asked as a relationship advisor and researcher is, "how can I find my soulmate?".

Admittedly, it is mostly women who ask me this, though I know many men would like to. They just don't want to admit it.

It seems to me that if we yearn for any type of love then it is 'soulmate love'. The idea that there is someone out there who is 'meant for us' is so powerful. It suggests some grand design at the centre of which is us. It signals that the most pure romantic love is within our reach, as is the possibility of lifetime happiness and contentment.

All very wonderful, exciting and optimistic; however, we should be careful what we wish for.

Soulmate love makes big demands on us.

We can define soulmate love as simply love from which there is no escape. It remains with us, to some degree, throughout our life. It contains little or no instrumentality or functionality, indeed it can sometimes appear to outsiders as quite irrational. Though to the two lovers it is the most natural state in the world. Soulmate loves are those that shake us to our very core. They are emotional earthquakes from which we will emerge somewhat different than before. This type of love does not merely change us, it can set us on an entirely different life path altogether. It is love without limits and without conditions. And it is love that demands self-sacrifice - whether you like it or not.

There is absolutely no point in me or anyone else suggesting when or where such loves might arise. It can be anywhere, anytime. You might be happily married and experiencing consensus love with your long-term partner, but then soulmate love comes along and bites you hard. What do you do then?

You might have been without a partner for years and without any expectations of a big love in your life, and then one evening, just out of curiosity, you decide to join an Internet dating agency. Within a few weeks your soulmate love has arrived in your life. Are you ready for what comes next?

You could meet this soulmate at university, on holiday, on the bus, in the library, at work. It could be a next-door neighbour, or someone who serves you coffee in your local Starbucks.

I know this will seem irrational to many people, but my own belief, based on decades of personal experience and observation, is that these soulmates are unavoidable in our life. If we are meant to meet him or her then we will do so. This love will come when it is ready and often when we least expect it. In spiritual terms, soulmate love is 'karma' - it (he or she) will come whatever. They are a central part of our life's love journey and we are meant to learn much from our experiences with them.

This unpredictability, unlooked for element, is one of the aspects to soulmate love that sets it apart from wishful love and consensus love. These latter two loves arise when we are seeking love, searching for it. Wishful love provides a temporary shelter and release from any deep emotional insecurity we are feeling at the time, while consensus love provides the emotional basis for a strong functional relationship with a long-term partner. Soulmate love may appear to offer us neither of these elements, it may not to fit into our lifestyle or future pathway, it may lack rationality and logic. However, trust it. If soulmate love has arrived in your life then the issue is not understanding why, but working out how you are going to cope with it.

Here is Max's story:

I am Scottish, aged 48 and ever since I was in my 20s I have been a player. By that I mean I had a lot of girlfriends and was really enjoying living the life, if you get my drift. My career was going well, money was no problem, and I got to travel lots of places. I'd been married once before, ten years previous, and had two young children from that relationship. Since that time I'd had a couple of live-in girlfriends but no one special. When May arrived in my life I think I was dating about four other women. She was 40 and single. Never been married, not had that many relationships actually. I didn't go looking for May she was someone I just happened to meet, quite by chance, at a local real estate agency, when I was looking to buy a new condo. At first she didn't interest me at all. But over the course of a few weeks we chatted and then dated. I had no intention of just seeing her and no one else. And I told her this. She knew there were other women in my life. Anyway, the relationship started but it took ages to kick off. We seemed to disagree about a lot. It took me a while to really understand her and she me. I think we must have 'split up' about four times over the first nine months. But for some reason we couldn't say goodbye. She would text me, or me her and off it went again. It took me a year to realise that I only wanted her. I stopped seeing other women and she moved in with me three years ago. The hardest thing for me has been the faithfulness bit. I occasionally played away even when we were first together, but it just didn't feel right. That was my sacrifice for the relationship; her sacrifice has been children: years ago I had a vasectomy and I am not interested in adopting; so no kids for us. I won't say it is easy, but I love her in such a deep way that I never, ever want us to be apart. No other woman comes even close. We have plans for the future, but really we have learned to take it day by day.

Imagine gripped by an invisible hand and nothing can release you from it. You may struggle and scream but it's not going away. This is how soulmate love attaches itself to us. And the more you struggle the tighter the grip becomes. In the end, you learn to live with it. Like Max, you learn how to make the adjustments to your life, the accommodations necessary to live in harmony with your soulmate.

And this point is important, just because they are your soulmate does not mean the relationship with them will always be peaceful. Precisely because we have so much emotional exposure in soulmate love so it can be fraught and stressful at times. In the example above, Max had to learn to be a different type of man if he and May were going to make it work. Just because they are soulmates does not make the relationship inevitable. They could split up in the future, though neither of them will ever fully get over their love for each other.

With soulmate love you have to just go with the flow of it; follow the path wherever it takes you both. Plans are pointless. Sure, consider the future, but the only issue is staying together. Come what may. This is not done out of deluded wishful love nor functional consensus love, it is done out of recognition that the relationship comes first; before family, friends, career, children, money, anything. Soulmate love is not instrumental; it is neither calculative nor expectant. It is simply a state of being in perfect unity with another soul, even when there are major lifestyle differences between you.

This is Paul's story:

Ged and I have been together for over twenty years now. We met at New York University and connected immediately. We are similar in so many ways; our value system, our sexual needs, how we see life actually. The big difference between us is in our leisure activities. I like to go to good restaurants, watch a movie, read a book, listen to some jazz. Ged is the sporty type; in fact he is a mountaineer. I know nothing about mountain climbing. Truthfully, a long walk in the country is my limit. He only started climbing about 15 years back, but then got really into it. He is very accomplished. Climbed in the Alps, the Himalayas, and many parts of North America. He is currently planning for Everest in two years time. I just have to let him go. I worry about him of course. And I miss him badly when he's away, but we can never leave each other. No other man has ever interested me. We have a totally monogamous relationship. We seem to have a connection with each other that is beyond understanding. A few years back he was climbing in Italy and had a very bad accident. Although I wasn't there at the time, actually thousands of miles away, I sensed something was wrong. I knew it. I tried to phone him but no answer. I was in a near state of panic, and then I got the phone call from the hospital to say he was ok. He was with other climbers at the time and they took care of him. It can be hard for me, but I accept that climbing is part of his life, part of who he is. The thing is, we have to be together. Life without each other is no life.

The compromise that Paul makes for the relationship is balanced by the compromise that Ged makes - Paul does not share his interest; there is this one fundamental aspect of their life together that requires understanding and a settlement. It emerged after they had started a relationship and they each have since had to make sacrifices to enable the relationship to continue.

One of the hardest tests we can face in love is when our soulmate arrives and yet we are already in a long-term relationship. If this happens then you need first to ensure that what you are feeling is not wishful love. That is, you not are secretly yearning for sexual or romantic excitement in your life simply because these elements are not present in your current relationship, perhaps a marriage. Wishful love, which is the love we are most likely to slip into in such circumstances, can meet the excitement criteria, but it is not soulmate love. Recognising what is happening to you is so important, but you need to be honest with yourself. A key question to ask is "will I leave my partner for my new love?" If the answer to this question is "yes", then next ask yourself what it is you want from this new lover. Are you prepared to be with them regardless of the consequences: e.g. family, children, career, money, home, friends? Again, if your love comes with conditions then this is not soulmate love. It may well be consensus love. Which is fine, but recognise it for what it is.

Only if you can answer three questions: "do I truly know this person I now love?"; will I leave my current relationship for them?"; and "will I accept the consequences whatever they might be?' with a clear "yes", does this suggest you are in soulmate love and emotionally strong enough to leave your current partner.

Is soulmate love always going to make you happy? No. There will be times when you are pulled in different directions, periods in your love relationship when other feelings and desires emerge.

Fran

Fran is a 61 year-old German woman. She has been married for thirty-five years and has two grown-up children. For the first twenty years of her marriage she devoted herself to the needs of her family. She was the archetypal 'mum'; never had a career, never really had a full-time job; she made sure the family came first, and her husband. But ten years ago she started to feel a little lost. The children were away at university, her husband had his own interests, and her marriage felt predictable and boring. Her sex life was non-existent and for a while she had a relationship with Karl, a man she met quite by chance at her local gym. This went on for six years, though her husband never found out, and she never told him. It was her secret. The affair was thrilling, romantic, sexual, and fulfilling. But it was never to last. She knew this in her heart. She would never leave her husband. Looking back now, Margaret has fond memories of her affair but accepts that she and her husband are soulmates and will be together for the remainder of their days.

Fran pulled back from exiting her marriage and has no regrets about that decision. Other people might have acted differently. Which tells us that soulmate love is not always for life. It can be or it might have a time limit. Fran could have moved on when she met Karl, but Karl was not her soulmate and she recognised that. Another person might have taken a different approach.

Annette

Annette is Norwegian, 52 years old and lives in Oslo. She is single and works in publishing. She has a 28 year old daughter. Annette was married at 20, and divorced at 44. Although she married young, Annette had met her soulmate. Her husband was 7 years older than her and she felt complete in their relationship. Getting married was, for her, the most natural thing to do. Annette never had a full time job during the marriage, preferring to be a housewife and mother.

The one aspect of her marriage that was not so satisfying was the sexual. Annette has a lot of sexual energy, but for the 24 years she was married she never had an orgasm with her husband. She had plenty alone, but not one with him. Annette was brought up in an age when wives didn't complain if their sexual needs were not being met. She considered herself a dutiful, faithful wife and tried to put aside that aspect of her being. When she was in her mid 30s, Annette went to university, doing firstly a BA and then an MA. This sparked a major period of change in her life. Her confidence grew but so did her feelings of frustration at her marriage, especially the lack of intimacy that had developed between her and her husband. Within a few years they were divorced. Annette now reflects on her marriage and tries hard not to be regretful that she didn't leave earlier. While splitting up with her husband was a time of great sadness and emotional pain she knew she had to move on. Yet she will also admit that he is her soulmate and she his. They remain good friends and keep in regular contact. They have a connection that transcends the sexual. There is no animosity between them. Annette now regularly dates men she meets either through her job or online. She is sexually expressive, emotionally satisfied, and living the type of independent life she could never have with her soulmate.

Would you give up your long-term soulmate in order to experience better sex, a more independent lifestyle, and freedom from the social convention that comes with marriage? I do not know, and maybe you don't either. You have to wait and see if you are ever in a such a situation. I am very familiar with couples that are soulmates, who have been together many years, raised a family together, but no longer have sex together. That aspect of intimacy went long ago; their relationship is now more akin to brother and sister, not lovers. Sometimes each partner takes a lover, but without revealing this to the other. Is this wrong, immoral, unfaithful, or deceitful? No, it is how they manage their relationship and if it works for them, then fine. Just because they have sex outside of the relationship doesn't mean they are no longer soulmates. I also know soulmate couples that separated after a few years of being together. The impact of their relationship remains with them, but their lives moved off in different directions and they felt compelled to follow.

Soulmate love: powerful, unavoidable, unpredictable and undoubtedly the most mysterious and difficult of any love to fully understand. This love we just have to go with. It seems to have its own agenda so let it take you where it will. It is not harmful. It will release its grip on you when it is ready, and invariably only when you are ready to move on. Do not assume that it will last a lifetime, or even that you will only have one soulmate love in your life. I know a number of people who have had two soulmate loves, though three is unlikely. In fact I think three would be just too debilitating for most of us.

Illusory Aspect: Very Low

Practical Aspect: Medium

Emotive Aspect: Very High

Long-term Prospect: Medium to Very High

Final thoughts on love

Love or no love, life is lived singularly

So, you fall in love and suddenly life is perfect. Wonderful experience and nothing quite like it. Well enjoy it as much as possible because this feeling won't last. The initial rush of emotion that comes when we find love is just too overwhelming, too forceful for us to be in it every day of our lives. It is not meant to be permanent. Also, you cannot wholly trust it. You might be out of this feeling within a few weeks. You will certainly come out of it eventually and then you are into the messy and much more difficult, but important business of nurturing the love long-term, that is if it is still there in your heart.

Love is work. It is a trek across a mountain range, not a walk in the park. You will have to struggle at times with your conflicting responses - especially if you've lived on your own for some years but then make the commitment to be with someone. In such a situation don't expect what comes next to be perfect. Life can be quite perfect when we are single and without a partner, it is much less likely to be perfect when we have to consider someone else and accommodate their needs in our lives. So no perfection - indeed, if it all seems perfect be suspicious because the chances are you haven't yet understood what is going on.

Also, be aware that love changes. Sometimes women, and men, say to me "yes, we are still in love but actually its now more like a brother-sister relationship'. Decipher this and what they are really saying is they are no longer having sex and yet they remain close, intimately entwined, maybe for the remainder of their lives. This is very common in long-term soulmate and consensus love relationships. The sex goes off in another direction, but the love remains. Actually, the love changes from dynamic, passionate, and maybe emotionally fraught, to being smooth, comfortable, reassuring but no longer passionate. And why not, who wants to be constantly immersed in some ongoing and highly stressful love battle with their partner? No one.

In all love relationships the ideal place to be is where the sex remains good, the passion strong, but the arguments have stopped. In other words, the immense emotional energy contained in the love between you comes out between the sheets. The remainder of the time you are just comfortable together; understanding and calm.

And don't be put off if there are lots of arguments between you during the first two or three years. This is entirely natural and so long as you avoid placing all the blame and responsibility on your partner, this period will pass and you'll emerge with a stronger relationship as a result.

The beginning of the love journey invariably begins with the words "I love you". In fact I consider these words fundamental - without them what do we have? Yet how many different people have said to you "I love you"? No doubt many, yet certainly not all of them meant it when they spoke these three most powerful words. Well, they might have felt they meant it at the time, but shortly afterwards and if they were honest with themselves, they will recognise it was said out of strong need, compassion, maybe a sense of responsibility, especially if you'd said it to them first.

We all have done this. Every one of us has said 'I love you' to someone and really it wasn't true. And I am no exception. So why did I say it?

Well, it wasn't for sex, because the sex was already happening. It was because I felt close and intimate with that person at that particular time, in that particular moment. There is a strong connection; a sense of intimacy, your feelings soar, and your heart goes out to your lover. You say "I love you" and feel you meant it, but when you look back you realise it wasn't love at all, it was warmth and closeness. The problem with the 'love' word is precisely its power. It is just too compelling.

I eventually realised what was happening in these moments and stopped myself from ever telling a woman I loved them unless I really did. And if I did say these words then for me that meant I could never easily let them go. We had to be together for an indeterminate time and we had to make it work as best we could - whatever the cost. So long as she felt the same way then the trek begins at that moment.

A lover may tell you they love me when you have been having sex together. Spiralling into that orgasmic peak they shout "I love you!". Fantastic experience, but don't imagine that it is love; it is just the emotional rush of it all.

Learn to hold back from saying "I love you" unless you really do. And if you are not sure whether you do or not, then you don't. The one thing about full-on love, whether it be wishful, consensus or soulmate, is that you'll know when you are in it.

What about the sex element in love, how do we cope with that? I am going to discuss sex and sexuality in Chapter 5, but one of the points to stress here is the difference between sex and love.

Sex, is a physical act, driven by a mental and hormonal response to a complex set of sexual and internalised erotic stimuli. Love is an emotional response to the actual or imagined identity of another person. The two, sex and love, usually go together, though the love can continue without the sex, and it is equally possible for the sex to continue without the love.

We can have fantastic sex with strangers; people we could and would never love. Women as well as men can do this. All that is needed is for the other person to push our 'erotic buttons'. It is a total fallacy to claim that women cannot have sex outside of love. Sure, many women will say this but they are only saying it in order to appear moral; there are still powerful social pressures on women to be 'good girls'.

And if you are in love and your lover has sex outside your relationship, does that automatically mean they do not love you anymore? Of course not; it may, but do not assume it. What is damaged in this moment is the trust and intimacy, sometimes built up over years. But it is just sex. Very, very few couples manage to stay together for decades without one or both partners having sex outside the relationship at some point. But this need not inevitably lead to the break-up of your relationship. You and your partner must recognise that, yes, it was just sex that occurred, not love.

If you have found love and its mutual, then hold on to it for as long as possible. Enjoy every moment of it, do not take it for granted and don't jump ship over minor issues, and sex can be a minor issue. You may not think so at the time, but the feeling of betrayal will pass. This can only come through forgiveness - both of you forgiving the other. Sure, be hurt and embrace that hurt, but then let it go. Love can overcome sexual infidelity, but sex alone can never replace love.

If you do not love yourself then you cannot fully love anyone else

Chapter 4: Your Relationships

"The biggest mistake is believing there is one right way to have a relationship" (D. Tannen)

It's a beautiful summer's day, the sun is shining and you are walking in the park. What do you see? You see young couples lying on the grass, arms around each other, surreptitiously kissing; you notice couples laughing as they play with their young children by the swings and slides; you walk past a retired older couple sitting on a park bench watching this world go by, smiling at each other in understanding and self-knowledge.

But, I say again, what exactly have you seen?

You probably thought you saw couples in love, happy and intimate. Well perhaps you did, or maybe not.

How many other partners have that young couple had and recently taken to that same park on a similar summer's day? Are the couple playing with their children blissfully happy or do they have other lovers in their lives? And the retired couple, well they have only recently met through a dating agency and this is their first meeting.

One of the most common misapprehensions is that love and relationships go together. We see couples, such as those in the park, and immediately we invest their relationship with the 'love discourse'; that is, we imagine they must be lovers, in love and happy. This is part of our natural human desire to socialise, associate, identify and thereby reinforce the social fabric of society. But the truth is we have no idea just what is actually going on in these relationships. In a way, we don't want to know, we much prefer to imagine it and thereby hold on to the myths of love, romance and Happy Ever After that we ourselves find so enticing.

But if we choose to look deeper, to divest ourselves of the impulse to posit all relationships as being about love, then much is revealed, not least about ourselves.

These are the aims of this chapter, to explain that not all relationships are about love; to identify the five main types of relationships; and to recognise that the vast majority of relationships come with a built-in time limit.

By recognising and accepting that not all relationships are alike, nor that they are all about love, then so we can recognise which type we might be in at any given time, which type we are attracted to, and which type we are really seeking.

Relationships are no longer for life they are for as long as the love lasts

1. The Peripheral Relationship

I love my friends I just don't want to live with them

What is the difference between a friendship and a relationship? Well, the friendship can be warm, comforting, intimate and companionable. What its not is demanding. You can come in and out of a friendship without too much emotional exposure. With a friendship you have not committed yourself in terms of sexual fidelity, having and raising children, sharing every aspect of your lives - you are not a couple. You will not talk long and hard with your friend about how they feel if you decide to live the other side of the world. You'll just up and go. You will not be emotionally upset if your friend has a lover, is married or, perhaps, is straight when you are gay. It is their affair, not yours.

Maybe you don't hear from your friend for a year or so, and then, quite unexpectedly, they suddenly pop up again in your life. Fine, you have lots to talk about. And if your friend has personal habits that you don't particularly like then it matters little - because you are not living with them as a partner. They have their way of living, as you have yours. You may love your friend, but as a friend. You are not and never will be, lovers.

So friendships and relationships are very different in many crucial respects. But, there is a middle space, between friend and partner. This is the 'peripheral relationship' and it is probably the most common of all relationships, especially today.

The peripheral relationship is marked by its lack of commitment. It is not central to your life, your future, who you are. It is warm, lovely and important, but it doesn't place heavy demands on you. It may very well be sexual, and the sex might be good, but it is not imbued with deep emotional passion. However, the absence of passion and intense emotion means this is an easy relationship to be in, and to be out of. The peripheral relationship can be taken up and put down with relative ease; it straddles the boundaries between friend and partner, even if you are having sex together on a regular basis.

We all need and should experience peripheral relationships at different points in our life's love journey. At the same time we should recognise them for what they are, and for what they are not. Their strength lies in the companionship and sharing which they can offer us, but they are not love relationships. You may love your 'peripheral lover' but more as a friend loves a friend, not as a soulmate loves a soulmate.

These relationships can arise anywhere. They may be someone you work with, who is married or in a committed relationship, but who yearns for some excitement outside of their marriage. So a casual affair begins. They can be individuals who meet, start dating, but come to accept that their relationship lacks sparkle and passion, but is important to them nonetheless. So they keep it going on that basis. Perhaps they are people who meet once, and then only rarely see each other again, but keep in touch through email. They can be friends who choose to cross the sex line, become occasional lovers, but really remain friends and not sexually committed to each other.

The peripheral relationship has a big plus - it is familiar and mostly without risk. These types of relationships are especially effective when the two people are able to share and talk about what is happening in their respective lives in a friendly and communicative way, without judgement or emotional exposure. The feelings for each other are there and such feelings are genuine, but these are not love relationships in the deepest sense of the term. There is an underpinning mutuality and understanding in peripheral relationships that makes them especially valuable in these days of distant social networking and singleton lifestyles. They are light, flexible, easy to hold on to, easy to let go of, and yet we can still learn from them.

These relationships work best when we are between 'big loves', when we want to feel close to someone but don't want to make a commitment. We don't intend to make any promises and we don't want any promises made to us. These are phases in our love journey when we just want someone close around us, who we can socialise and share aspects of our life with, not someone making big demands or trying to push us into a particular lifestyle or major obligation. We may be finding ourselves again after a big love has ended painfully; we are going slowly forward, testing the relationship waters to see how inviting they feel; not jumping in too quickly. The peripheral relationship is perfect in such circumstances. You can share your feelings and expectations and make particular accommodations; negotiate some flexibility and agreements though not enough to make you feel uneasy or anxious. So it is fundamentally about convenience, not commitment. And everyone recognises and is fine with that distinction.

The peripheral relationship is only risky when we mistake it for more than it is or more than it can possibly be - or if our partner does. In such situations so we are into the land of love delusion and there lies many potential dangers. Someone is going to get hurt. And the person most risk is the one who has failed to recognise that this is, actually, a peripheral relationship, not a soulmate relationship, or even a consensual love affair. It is not going anywhere. It has no future beyond what it is now.

Often, our awareness that we are in a peripheral relationship can take time. It arises slowly. By that I mean we can easily begin a relationship imagining or hoping this could be a big one and perhaps it feels like that for a short period, but it turns out to be comfortable, not sparkling. We are not in love with this person and never will be.

At that point go back to the advice I give in the chapter above which is to avoid at all costs telling your partner that you love them. Do not say this out of obligation or duty. Do not say it just because they want to hear those words from you. Do not place unattainable expectations on the peripheral relationship, or your partner, because if you do then you are creating an illusion the outcome of which will surely be hurt and pain for one or both of you.

Sex is pleasure, love is responsibility

Welcome the times when a peripheral relationship enters your life. For these relationships can last, they can weather many storms, they can go from sexual to platonic quite easily and without recrimination or regret. They are not burdened by unrealistic hope, unmitigated desire, or the myths of Happy Ever After. They are what they are and that is their greatest strength and attraction. So long as you recognise and accept this, and do not attempt to force them into being something they can never be, then you'll be fine.

Finally, do not make the mistake of diminishing these types of relationships. We learn from all our relationships and the peripheral one is no exception. Indeed, this type of relationship is probably the safest and most secure of all in terms of learning about our selves but with the minimum of emotional exposure and risk.

Most common type of love associated with this relationship: wishful love and consensus love.

Example:

Jess and Rob are in their 40s. Both are divorced, have children from previous relationships and live and work in London. Jess is a school administrator. Rob is a self-employed printer. When they are not working they are usually involved in looking after their respective children. Although they have been seeing each other for two years now, they have no intention of moving in together. They each have their own homes, circle of friends and their weekends are often taken up with childcare duties. They try and see each other a couple of times a week but there is no routine. Their lives are full and satisfying, if at times a little stressful. Jess has been divorced now for ten years, Rob for five. They have each had relationships in the past and at times quite intense ones, but right now, with their work and parenting commitments, they are not seeking anything more than the supportive, flexible and casual relationship they have with each other. Neither is involved with anyone else and in many respects they appear the archetypal stable and settled couple. At the same time, Jess and Rob do not make any promises to each other about the future. They are very relaxed about the way their relationship has developed and neither puts pressure on the other to make it more than it is.

2. The Draining Relationship

Some people are relationship vampires. They nourish themselves on the love of others but give little in return

The easiest, most beneficial and certainly most empowering relationships to be in are those with balance. That is, the expectations of what each person contributes are understood and this is followed up in practice. This does not necessarily mean there is no flexibility, but it does mean that materially and emotionally neither partner is draining from the other. There is a mutuality which remains fairly constant throughout the life of the relationship and which is enabling for both individuals.

One way to appreciate the importance of this rule is to recognise that all intimate relationships are invested with their unique energy. What each person brings to the relationship has a quality of energy about it; we each have our own energy or emotional presence and this inevitably gets transferred to relationships. This energy can be positive or it can be negative, though most of us experience and emit positive and negative energy at different times, depending on our mood, how stressed we are, and our general level of health and well-being. However, for some individuals negative energy is always around them and this can create risks for their loved ones. For example, if one person is wholly passive while the other is constantly impatient, angry and aggressive then clearly there is a crucial energy imbalance. Similarly, if one person lacks empathy and is selfish, puts themselves first in every situation, while the other partner acquiesces in this arrangement thereby being marginalised and diminished, then, again, the relationship is draining and out of kilter.

Basically, in a draining relationship, one person is giving while the other is doing the taking. One partner is elevated and empowered but at the price of the other partner being lessened and reduced. Sometimes the 'taking' partner may be aware of their actions, though often they are not. The reason for this lack of self-awareness can be because they have been adopting such an approach to all their relationships and over many years, perhaps emulating it from how they experienced their upbringing, for example. For them, it's just the 'way they are'. However, for the person who is being drained of energy and love then it is a serious and potentially dangerous state to be in.

In the most extreme draining relationships one can find violence and aggression by one partner towards the other. In these relationships the emotional work and energy required to continue as the abused party in the relationship is massive and debilitating. Such relationships come to exist in an ongoing culture of anxiety and insecurity for one person, while the other feels stronger and more secure through their ability to draw energy from the 'weaker' partner.

Such relationships can also contain emotional and physical blackmail; e.g. where one partner in the relationship threatens to commit suicide if their partner leaves them. Or a partner threatening bodily harm to their partner, children, other family members, if that partner does not do as they ask or if they try and leave.

Milder, but also unbalanced draining relationships can exist where there is a significant intellectual or social differentiation between the parties. For example, if one partner is middle class and educated, while the other partner is uneducated and working class, so an imbalance can arise in which intellectual, social and class differences become a serious issue. These may not be apparent early on in the relationship, but they can become a major problem as time passes. Typically, this can involve one person feeling silenced and ignored, not understood, valued, appreciated or respected. Consequently, they experience slow but steady erosion in self-esteem and confidence.

Imbalance can arise in any number of ways; one partner can sense a deep need and insecurity in the other and they take advantage of this to act in a dominant and unsympathetic manner. An example here might be the dominant partner having numerous sexual liaisons and not attempting to hide this fact. Imbalance can often arise through money and material possessions; e.g. one partner is the sole breadwinner and dictates how much the other partner should receive in 'allowance' each month and controls this very strictly and with an attitude of superiority.

Conversely, one partner can drain the other of emotional energy by being overly passive and appearing constantly needy, forever presenting themselves as vulnerable, insecure, and requiring attention. But no matter how much attention and love they receive, it is never enough and the 'blame' for this 'lack of love' is always laid a the door of their partner.

While it is true that 'opposites attract' it is also true that similarities between partners make for the stronger relationships. While it is not necessary for a relationship to work for the partners to be alike, they should have empathy, respect and appreciation for each other's differences. Where they are of opposite character and personality, as can often be the case, then it makes balance even more critical, not less. The ways such balance can be achieved are numerous and I discuss some of them in Chapter 6, but they certainly include open communication, listening, and the sharing of emotions and feelings but without recrimination, anger and violent response. The overall context for developing such an enabling relationship concerns control; that is, neither partner should attempt to control the other either through threat, coercion, emotional blackmail or aggressive behaviour.

If you are not in a draining relationship, and have never experienced one, then you may reasonably ask why the drained party continues to stay. As I say above, this could be because that person is seriously, and justifiably, concerned for their physical safety, or that of their children, should they try and leave. But it can also be because draining relationships have a certain addictive quality. For those individuals who already have extremely low self-esteem and confidence prior to starting the relationship, and perhaps have experienced imbalanced relationships in the past (often through their immediate family), then to be in a relationship with a strongly dominant partner, especially one who constantly says "I love you", can be a real attraction. In a perverse way, the inherent imbalance almost feels 'normal' to the drained partner thereby 'validating' how they see have come to see themselves as a man or woman.

Many people who are on the receiving end of a draining relationship will say that for a long time they felt the guilty party. They really believed their inadequacies were the reason their partner was controlling or even abusive. They reasoned that if only they could love their partner more then h/she would become a nicer person, easier to be with, less dictatorial.

The truth is, however, that love is not the problem here. It is the mental attitude and character of, usually, the dominating party, but also, of course, the overly passive response of the other partner. Both contribute, though it is the domineering partner who must reflect on their actions and desist if they can. Love, on its own, is not enough to break the cycle of decline which relationship is in. This cycle can only be broken by the actions of both parties - mutual reflection, calm and appreciative understanding, and, often, counselling by a neutral third party.

Unfortunately, while draining relationships are damaging and exhausting, they can go on for a long time. The pattern of behaviour, whereby one partner exercises dominance and control over the other, reinforced through expressions of love and need, gets embedded through the years, becomes subtle and sophisticated in its expression and, for both parties, experienced as their 'relationship normality'.

However, there are two, very different, 'break points' that often arise in such relationships. The first, and most dramatic, is when the dominated partner reaches their own particular breaking point and leaves, having come to the conclusion that to stay in the relationship is just asking too much of themselves and/or their children. They recognise that to continue is intolerable, in which case it is better to go now and deal with the consequences rather than allow the situation to persist any longer. The second break point, or trigger for leaving, is when the dominated partner experiences a significant increase in their confidence and self-esteem. This can come about in a number of different ways but invariably involves experiences outside the relationship, for example; going on to further or higher education and achieving success as a mature student; finding a lover outside the relationship who is very understanding and supportive; or experiencing an improvement in their career prospects and consequently a strengthening of their self-esteem and confidence.

Most common type of love associated with this relationship: wishful love

Example:

Lisa is aged 39. She is British and lives in Birmingham with her husband and 17 year old son. She is very happy. Her seven year long relationship is strong, loving and balanced. Lisa appreciates the relationship she has because her first experiences of 'love' were

very different. At the age of 17 Lisa got into a relationship with a 35 year old man. Lisa was at college, struggling with money and her own family relationships, which were, as she puts it, "toxic" (Lisa is a adopted and she experienced a lot of emotional turmoil during childhood). This relationship with the older man appeared to be perfect - it promised security, love, and the protection of an experienced male. Lisa moved in with her lover and in the beginning it was "blissful". But then it changed. Her lover became firstly emotionally abusive, domineering and controlling, and then eventually he became violent. Lisa struggled hard to cope. She felt she was in the wrong, that somehow she had to love him more so that he would recognise that love and love her more strongly in return. She felt guilty and inadequate. Her confidence dropped, her self-worth plummeted. She had no one to turn to. She rarely went anywhere without her partner and she had no close friends. This situation lasted for six years, during which she got pregnant with her son. One day, while her partner was out at work, she just packed her bags and went with her son to a local shelter for homeless women. They took her and her son in. She eventually found work and her life and confidence, improved. In her late 20s she returned to college, did an Access course, and then on to university where she did a degree. Very tentatively she went back into dating men. She met her future husband through friends.

3. The Functional Relationship

We treasure our individuality we just don't want to always be alone with it

I know its something we hate to admit but the truth is all relationships have a degree of pragmatism about them. Even if we have a soulmate, having a relationship with that person is more demanding than simply loving them. All relationships work best when they contain a good level of realism, balance and self-awareness. We should also acknowledge that love can often feel strongest when it is at a distance, removed from the everyday practicalities and often tedious, sometimes stressful, business of being in a relationship, especially one which involves living together as a couple. In such situations the love, and the person who is our love interest, is invested with a certain mythical or fantasy quality that heightens its hold on our emotions. But, as I have stressed above, myths do not help relationships to last. Ultimately the fantasy balloon will deflate.

However, there are relationships that are built not so much on love, but on hard-headed realism. They are functional, pragmatic and instrumental. They exist almost entirely on an understood social or financial arrangement that suits both parties. The most obvious examples are arranged marriages, and these remain very common worldwide, especially in societies that use marriage as a way of building up family dynasties and ensuring economic stability for middle-class couples especially.

The big strength of these relationships is, of course, the aspect entirely missing from the draining relationship - that of balance. A functional relationship can only exist so long as the factors that enabled it to come into existence in the first place are maintained. And this itself creates the balance; these are trade-offs that signal what each party brings to the arrangement, and I give examples of such trade-offs below. Invariably, financial and material prosperity are at the heart of most functional relationships. Further key aspects often include health and physical well-being, personal security, having and raising children, even residency in a foreign country.

Are such relationships never about love? Well, that depends on how they evolve over time and I discuss this below. As I explain, even the most pragmatically driven functional relationship can evolve into a 'formative relationship', one that contains a strong element of deep affection, if not love. Indeed, I know from talking to many men and women in Asia, those expecting to go into an arranged marriage or already in one, that they carry a big hope the functional side will eventually be replaced by love and desire.

Aside from the more obvious arranged marriage, what other examples of a functional relationship are there? Well I see a lot of functional relationships in Thailand, indeed across Asia, ones that are not formally arranged by a family, but sustained by clearly marked roles and expectations. Invariably such relationships exist around a quite traditional male and female division of labour whereby the man is the main provider and the woman the nurturer and carer, though the opposite can occur.

If you are Western and you come to Thailand as a visitor, one of the things that will strike you very quickly are the numerous older Western men with younger Asian women. You will look at these men and you may well consider them unattractive as relationship material. Yet they are often with quite beautiful and desirable young women, women they could never hope to attract back home in the West. Your first reaction will be to presume the women must be with these men for money. Well, that may be true in part, though it would be a mistake to assume all these women are sex workers; many are, but equally many are not. And it would be a mistake to assume all these women are poor and uneducated. My own wife, who is Thai, is a scientist, has an MA in physics from a German university and comes from a family which has three members with PhDs. Her father was for many years a Pro-Vice Chancellor of a major Thai university.

So what is going on here? What you are seeing are mostly, though not exclusively, functional relationships, whereby the Western man is providing financial security, social status, and perhaps children and a family, for the woman. If he is older, as most of these men are, then that is a big plus for the relationship as the woman will consider him to be more stable, more settled.

Indeed, Western men who are retired and have a regular income through a pension for example, are especially sought after in Asia. They are much less likely to be what the Asian women call 'butterflies'; men who flit from woman to woman.

The trade-off is that in return for a home and financial security, the woman provides intimate companionship, residential security in Thailand or wherever, general homecare and emotional and physical support; the latter aspect being increasingly important as the man gets older. So appealing is this functional arrangement for both parties that there are now estimated to be well over 100,000 Westerners living in Thailand alone, most of which will be in relationships or married to, Thai women. Many more Western men live in Cambodia, China, Singapore, Hong Kong and Taiwan and are married to, or in committed relationships with, usually much younger, local women.

The issues that can readily arise in cross-cultural relationships such as these are numerous and really worthy of a separate book altogether. However, we should not assume these functional relationships to inevitably be brief ones. I know of several Thai-Western marriages that are still going strong after 25 years or more, though also of many more which lasted only a few months.

The big danger to all functional relationships, cross-cultural or not, is the absence of any awareness that they are, indeed, functional. If one or both partners fail to recognise and accept that there is a functional element at work in the relationship, indeed which probably renders the relationship into existence in the first place, then when this realisation does occur, as surely it will, they are in for a major emotional shock. They will feel hurt, deceived, manipulated and damaged. It is very hard to come back from this position and 'forgive' their partner, or perhaps, themselves, the reason being that the feeling of trust has gone. As I stress in my penultimate chapter, self-awareness is so key to modern relationships, as is recognising that love itself is not immune to illusion.

Because functional relationships are most likely to occur where there is material need, especially need for financial security and physical caring, they are particularly common between individuals of different social and economic backgrounds, e.g. where the man is relatively wealthy and the woman not. However, we should resist the temptation to adopt a judgemental attitude towards such relationships. If we are sitting comfortably in our rather privileged social or cultural environment then it can be difficult to appreciate just how appealing a functional relationship is for people less secure than ourselves. It is also important to recognise that, for many individuals, the functional relationship can appear much more attractive than one based solely on love. Often one finds that older men and women, who have had big love relationships in the past and found they floundered for whatever reason, come to adopt a more pragmatic attitude as they get older. They see love as temporary and risky emotion to invest one's future in. Much better to invest one's future in a relationship built on hard-headed pragmatism and material realism. They realise they have some control over the material, if not the emotional.

In the West one can see many examples of this with older, retired people especially. These couples may be very similar in terms of financial status, class and social background, but the love is less important than the fact that they can support each other health-wise, and financially, as they get older. These are functional relationships and they work very well indeed. To be sure, there needs to be affection between the couple for the relationship to be truly beneficial, but love itself, or the lack of it, need not be a major factor. What is the key element is the ability of the couple to live together in harmony and understanding. Love does not necessarily bring harmony, indeed it can and does often bring the opposite, especially if it is accompanied by unrealistic expectations.

Finally, what of the increasing number of marriages that have pre-nuptial agreements? Are these entirely functional relationships? Well, they are certainly underpinned by a strong element of pragmatism, and, indeed, material protection. Otherwise why have the agreement in the first place? In this respect they are functional in essence, though we should not assume they are not motivated by love. They are, however, illustrative of the individualism at the heart of all societies and cultures. The functional relationship, ultimately, symbolises a hard truth, which is that 'in love' or not, in the final reckoning we are on our own.

Most common type of love associated with this relationship: consensus love.

Example:

Maple and Frank are both in their mid 60s. They are married and live in the seaside town of Blackpool, in the north of England. Maple and Frank have each been married before and have grown up children and grandchildren, now living around the world. They met ten years ago, when both were members of a group of countryside walkers. Maple and Frank love the Lake District in northern England and still drive up there to go walking on the fells. They keep fit and active. They have each had big love relationships in the past; Frank's first wife died of cancer when she was 32. He married a second time, had two more children in that relationship, and then got divorced in his late 40s. Maple was first married at 21 and that relationship last 27 years, until her divorce. She loved her first husband, he was her soulmate, and Maple had decided never to marry again. But after meeting Frank and them getting on so well together, Maple realised it would be better to go into old age with a friend and companion - someone to share her life with and who could take care of her as she aged. Frank felt exactly the same about Maple and so they sold their respective homes, bought a trim semi-detached home in Blackpool, and got married eight years ago. Being married is, for them, not the same as it was in their younger days. They don't feel the pressure of having to work, pay a mortgage, raise children, or indeed be in love. They are intimate and comfortable together. The love they have has grown out of that companionship. And of course there is the financial reality - they are each able to provide for the other and when one of them passes on so the other will have a home and pension income for the rest of their life.

4. The Full-Love Relationship

As far as sexual relationships are concerned there is no such thing as unconditional love

As I have emphasised, not all relationships need be about love, indeed in many relationships love is either pretty much absent from the start or has been replaced by companionship, friendship, mutual understanding and empathy. This doesn't make the relationship necessarily weaker; very often those relationships that are entirely functional are strong and stable. It just that they are not built on love.

That said, love is a major emotional factor in most relationships; whether it be wishful love, consensus love or soulmate love. In this section I want to describe the 'full-love relationship'. For me, this relationship is one most commonly underpinned by soulmate love, though it can be applicable to consensus love depending on the formative way the love has developed over time.

The full-love relationship is one that only works or comes into existence if the feelings are mutual between both partners. If one person feels the love strongly while the other is less sure or indeed only claiming to be in love so as to not hurt the feelings of the other, then this is not a full-love relationship. It is either a peripheral, functional or draining relationship. Often we don't realise this until we are well into the relationship - that is, we enter into it believing we are in love and our partner loves us, only to eventually realise the love was never really there at all.

In the full-love relationship the love is there from the beginning, or very early on. It is clear, unambiguous and powerful. These types of relationships are the ones most of us are seeking and want to experience during our life's love journey, though, again, there are times when a peripheral or functional relationship might suit us better.

The risky assumption with any full-love relationship is that the strength of the love will see you through, whatever comes along. It won't. Declaring our undying love for someone, and feeling that commitment in every fibre of our being, isn't enough. Love on its own does not bring understanding, communication, reflection and eternal desire. As I go on to explain in the next chapter, these are just some of the important dynamics that go to make up 'togetherness' and they have to be worked at. The truth is, we can be very happy in our togetherness with a partner we don't love passionately, but with whom we can comfortably and easily live every day of our lives.

Full-love relationships can end, just like any relationship. In fact, the average length of time for all relationships is much less than ten years, even full love ones. At the same time, there is a sense of purity to the full-love relationship, untarnished as it is by undue pragmatism, illusion or an imbalance of power between the couple. In which case the prospects for such a relationship lasting are good. And these types of relationships are certainly worth holding on to and working at. They don't come around that often. Its much easier, for example, to get into a peripheral relationship, or even a draining one, than it is a full-love one, simply because the emotional wave which overwhelms us in such a relationship is heightened by the realisation that we are loved equally in return. The duality of the love is the key to it. It is never enough that we love someone; that love must be reciprocated for any relationship to work, and in a full-love relationship it is.

The big difference, then, between a full-love relationship and any other type is that critical aspect of mutual feeling and expression of declared and realised love. The most common type of love that therefore becomes associated with a full love relationship is soulmate love, and I have described that in some detail above.

But to reiterate, soulmate love is a love that comes unbidden and unexpectedly. It is immensely powerful and will impact on us in every aspect of our lives. I tend towards seeing soulmate love as ultimately positive and benign. Even after we have come out of such a relationship, divorced for example, the memories of our time with our soulmate will remain with us throughout our lives, and so long as we can move on from such a relationship with feelings of warmth towards our ex-partner, those memories will not be painful.

The other critical aspect is that it is never the case that just one person is the soulmate. Both must be soulmates to each other if it is truly soulmate love. Again, this emphasises the shared love that needs to be present in a full-love relationship. It is full love precisely because both partners are contributing to it, feeling it, and committed to it.

So what can you expect from a full-love relationship?

Let me deal with the harder aspects first. The full-love relationship is emotionally demanding, exposes you to the risk of deep hurt and will not necessarily be smooth. With love so too comes expectation, indeed the real hope of Happy

Ever After. The point is, however, not to be happy ever after, but to be content today. And being content inevitably means accepting that the relationship will make its demands on you and not being fazed when such turbulence comes along. As I discuss in the penultimate chapter, all relationships have their unique dynamic, energy, and identity. This arises from the contribution which both parties make to it, and, of course, any other key influences, not least parents, in-laws, children, and so on. The full-love relationship is more risky precisely because it is underpinned by emotion and deep feeling, and much less by the pragmatism of, say, a functional relationship.

Start with shared love, add in all our hopes and dreams, stir it up with the external variables that we have little control over, and you clearly have a volatile and emotive mix.

There is a further factor which is most important in understanding full-love relationships and which is especially pertinent in the 21st century, and that is our desire for the perfect or 'pure' relationship.

The notion of the pure relationship links with our sense of individuality and our desire for intimacy and trust. It is defined by our ongoing pursuit of personal happiness, the belief that we are entitled to this happiness in which case we should not let anything or anyone get in the way of us achieving it. However, whether this pursuit is reasonable or not, the truth is we live in an age of uncertainty, made so not least by globalisation, new technology and an erasing or questioning of many of our assumptions about the future. Not unreasonably, all this can create real angst in people. On one hand we are unsure about the future, and at the same time we are dedicated to the pursuit of happiness. The paradox is obvious and inevitably a source of tension in all 21st century full-love relationships.

The pursuit of individual happiness and a pure relationship to define it places enormous demands on us and on our love relationships. We are increasingly prone to individualisation, pursing our own life journey; our personal happiness project. Yet we hope that someone else can provide the trust, intimacy and emotional environment to make that project work. This raises a simple question: if we are ultimately on our own whom can we truly share this journey with - whom can we trust to bring us happiness?

As I described in earlier chapters, in past centuries the world appeared simpler, more manageable and predictable. In the 21st century the world appears anything but simple, fairly unmanageable, and certainly not predictable. But there is still our hope that we can alleviate some of this uncertainly by having a soulmate with us in a full-love relationship. Such relationships appear, then, the most pure, the most ideal. Which is why we hope for them.

Crucially, the full-love relationship, whether it is underpinned by soulmate love or not, is ultimately defined by trust and shared intimacy. This is what gives it the purity - it appears uncorrupted by everyday life and living. It is elevated beyond the normal, to become almost supernatural.

So the trust factor is not merely the glue that holds the relationship together, it is the very justification for the relationship in the first place. I trust my lover and they trust me, in which case we can go forward into this relationship secure in the knowledge that what we have is pure and eternal. We tell ourselves we can commit to this relationship in the real hope that it will further our individual pursuit of happiness. It will alleviate our own angst about the future; settle our inner unease regarding this unpredictable and fluid world we are living in.

The problem of course, is that trust is vulnerable. It only takes one breach of that trust for us to question the whole value and purpose of the relationship. And if that trust contract is broken then it can seem to us that there is no point in continuing, in which case we say 'no more'. This is one of the major reasons why many relationships breakdown, especially full-love ones.

You might consider the full-love relationship to be just too risky. You may not relish being emotionally exposed, trusting your happiness and contentment to another person. You may be wary of the pain that can come from losing such a love.

Well against that possibility you have to set the fact that full-love relationships are the most emotionally rewarding and satisfying of any. They help define our lives, and come to inform our very identity; they influence not only who we are today but also whom we can be in tomorrow. With full-love relationships we are touching the very essence of what is good and possible in terms of intimate and sexual togetherness with another being. Full-loves are the pinnacle of all relationships, especially when they are driven by soulmate love. Consequently, they are not to be taken lightly, nor approached in a blasé manner. For those of us of a religious persuasion, they are a gift of God. And for those of us without any God, the full-love relationship provides a powerful alternative.

My advice is twofold: firstly if your soulmate comes along and you both want to create a relationship from this love, then go for it. Life is short and nothing is gained without risk. Sure, your life's love journey will be a roller-coaster at times, but sitting and watching other people go by on theirs is not nearly as exciting or rewarding as being on the ride yourself. Secondly, don't go into the relationship expecting it to be perfect and don't rush out of it if the trust contract ever gets breached; work at revising the contract not ending the relationship.

Most common type of love associated with the full-love relationship: soulmate love and consensus love.

Example:

Doreen and Len were 28 when they married, shortly after the end of the 2nd World War. He had served in the Royal Navy from the age of 17 she had always worked but never had a career. Both left school at 14. They met in Margate, England, in 1943, during one of the spells when Len was on leave. For both, it was a full love relationship from the start. Neither had experienced anything similar in their lives and really it didn't take them long to realise they wanted to get married and live the rest of their lives together. They waited until the war was over and then married. Len left the Royal Navy and they opened a small grocers store in Margate. They lived above the shop. Life was not easy. Food rationing was still in place and this didn't end until 1954. They had few luxuries though did manage to buy a small van. Their first child, Simon, came along in 1950. Their second, Elaine, was born five years later. By the time they reached their late 40s, Doreen and Len had successfully established their business, seen their children through schooling, and worked hard together as a couple. The love had changed somewhat over the decades and while it was still there, the passion was not. At the age of 51, Len began a relationship with another woman. He managed to keep this affair secret for a while, but he was not an emotionally strong man and eventually he felt compelled to reveal all to Doreen. Doreen was extremely hurt, but forgave Len. However, Len never forgave himself and shortly afterwards he left to live on his own. They were divorced five years later. Len remarried, Doreen never did. For both, their full love relationship together was the only one they were going to experience in their lives. They were together for over 20 years, though their love for each other really never died. Doreen died in 2009. Len passed away shortly afterwards.

5. The Changing Relationship

If we didn't have mirrors how would we know we'd changed?

This is not so much a type of relationship as the reality within all relationships. To some degree or another, all relationships are formative. That is, they are a process not an outcome. There is never an end point to a relationship so long as it continues. The end point only comes when one of us dies or we split up. So recognise that whatever type of relationship you are in, or are seeking, there is an ongoing momentum to it that cannot be fully controlled and certainly not predicted. We have to be *in* relationships. We cannot claim we *have* a relationship in the same way we have a car or a house. So being in a relationship means going with the flow of it, not assuming, for example, that by getting married we are giving the relationship a final, total and secure stability. Marriage cannot do that, indeed it never could.

So the 'changing relationship' is one we will all have, whether we are in a functional, draining, peripheral or full-love type. Change and movement is crucial to life, it is fundamental to living, and it is elementary to our identity. So expect it in your relationships.

Is change more likely in some relationships than others?

Well, I believe that the draining relationship is the most difficult to change, as well as being the most debilitating to be in. Some relationships don't start out like this but for different reasons this is what they evolve into. Unless the person who is the 'leech' (i.e. doing the draining) becomes aware of their actions and the consequences for the relationship, then so it will continue. External counselling can help in such situations otherwise the only advice is to leave. Ultimately the person who is being 'drained' of love and emotional security must come to realise that this is neither healthy nor beneficial to them. Leaving is the only solution.

The peripheral relationship can move on to become a full-love relationship in some situations and certainly I wouldn't rule this out as a possibility. However, this takes both parties to make it happen which can only occur when each feels mutual love for each other - e.g. have gone beyond the friendship zone that previously defined their peripheral relationship. I have seen this happen with couples, but usually this has been due to the fact that they failed to recognise in the initial stages that they were, in fact, soulmates. For example, early on into their relationship one or both of the parties were continuing to see other people and therefore viewed their mutual relationship as a peripheral one. Then the reality slowly dawns that they are actually in love and deeply. At that point they move from a peripheral into a full-love relationship.

Functional relationships tend to be very stable, but only so long as the factors that ensured the stability and functionality from the start, remain in place. For example, if the relationship is built around one partner being the primary breadwinner, can it survive that person being made unemployed? If the functionality assumes no children, what happens if children come along? And if one partner considers the beauty of the other to be a major reason why they are with them (e.g. the 'trophy wife' syndrome), then can the relationship survive loss of beauty and ageing?

For the full-love relationship change can come about through shifts in the identity and expectations of the partners. We can start out loving our partner, and they us, but over many years the love changes to become less intense, less exciting. What emerges is more of a functional arrangement, whereby the couple still have love for each other, but sexual desire, for example, has disappeared. This does not inevitably herald a split, and I have seen many couples continue contentedly in such situations. What has happened is that, over time, a functional dimension has crept into the relationship and which can be illustrated by any number of rational considerations; e.g. the wish to raise children in a nuclear family environment, not as a single parent; the need to stay together and not therefore risk financial meltdown through divorce; the desire to keep up social appearances; the intention to care for one partner who may be experiencing serious health problems. All these and countless other factors can hold a full-love relationship together and long after the fires of love have cooled.

All relationships, whatever their origin or type, have the potential to provide us with a feeling of association and belonging. That is how they work, and that is why we enter into them. No one goes into a relationship hoping to be lonely. All of us enter into relationships out of optimism and hope; seeking companionship, friendship, security and/or love. This truth tells us how important are intimate relationships not only for us, but for society.

Whatever change happens hold on to your optimism and hope - because the journey continues.

When it comes to relationships, ten years is a life-time

Chapter 5: Sex and Pleasure

6.5 billion people and each one started out with an orgasm

The problem with sex?

More relationships come to grief over sex than any other single factor. Why does this happen? Well, the reasons are numerous but they usually come down to one common factor: we have failed to be grown up about sex and especially our own sexuality. We invest so much in the pursuit of sex, yet we can never wholly control it. Inevitably, our sexual desires prove stronger than the social codes that demand we are 'good'.

This leads to us living what Italian sociologist, Syliva Gherardi, terms a 'schizogenic' existence - whereby we constantly have to present ourselves in particular but contrasting ways so as to be 'accepted' and deemed 'normal' by different sections of society; so women managers, for example have to become adept at performing masculinity in the workplace while still presenting themselves as overtly feminine. In such situations, individuals end up not only living out multiple identities, some of which are in conflict with each other, but also displacing their true feelings. As I go on to reveal in this chapter, both men and women can be very accomplished at hiding their true feelings when it comes to sex. This may be clever, but is it healthy for relationships - is it healthy for us? I think not.

The contradictions between sexual expectation and sexual reality are legion. For example, why do we continue to assume that people are going to remain faithful in relationships? Most are not, especially those in long-term relationships. Why do we believe men are the ones driven by sexual urges that lead them to being unfaithful? All the evidence shows that women are, now, increasingly likely to 'play away' especially if they are unhappy and unsatisfied in the physical side of their relationship. Why do we assume that our sexual needs are going to remain constant throughout our lives? This is just not true. Just as we change over the years, so does our sexuality. And certainly do not buy into the myth that age diminishes desire. The older age group is not now called the 'swinging sixties' for nothing. Teenagers will first have sex at, say, fifteen, but if they think all bedroom activities will cease once they get past forty, or even fifty, then they are very mistaken. They have a lot to look forward to.

Sex is a skill - it needs to be learnt and we need to practice it often so as to become adept. It is not a skill to be practiced on one's own

Sexuality is a powerful drive in each of us, but so long as we pretend we can control it simply by saying, "I do" or "I love you," then we are always going to be picking up the pieces some years later.

This inability of ours to accept something so basic about human beings, so fundamental to adulthood, is one of the reasons we are unable to hold our relationships together. We have to deal with this, and in a mature and open way. We are attempting to build long-term relationships on a myth. The myth being that men, and women, can control their sexual needs through either guilt, fear or through commitment and love for their partner. This is a dangerous delusion. Most of us cannot do this. And trying to do it just creates real psychological damage in us. It is like trying not to masturbate as a teenager out of fear that it is somehow 'unnatural.' And when we can no longer control our desires we 'succumb,' and this brings even more problems, not least guilt, lies, and shame.

How many of your married friends are having, or had, affairs, secret liaisons? Many, and probably more than you realize. Indeed, it is quite possible you have yourself or your own partner has. Don't feel bad or guilty - this goes on everywhere. But we don't like to admit it. We are trapped between what we feel is expected of us, and what we feel emotionally and sexually deep inside. The result is oceans of unmitigated guilt and pain. There are millions of people living their lives while totting the most unmanageable guilt and pain baggage over illicit sex. Let it go! Release yourself from the burden. You will feel a lot better for doing so.

The truth is we are not yet fully mature when it comes to sex. At least society isn't. Most societies, including 'modern' ones like the USA and UK are deeply sexually conservative. Of course, millions of individuals are more open-minded, but then they are forced to conceal their sexual activities and desires in order not to receive negative judgments from the community they live in.

Very few of us can have sex with only one person for decade after decade. This is a truth that every man knows, though few will ever admit it and certainly not to their wife or partner. Yes, I know, many women will say that they cannot have sex with someone they don't love. Not true. Don't believe it. Women who say this are just in denial. Women can have sex for pleasure just like men can. And increasingly they are doing. Holding on to this 'sexual ideal' has always been problematic, but in the 21st century, when people travel and communicate so much more quickly and readily, it has become a major issue in relationships.

Most relationships eventually have to confront the big question: do we cheat and keep it secret or do we commit to ethical non-monogamy? Be very careful how you answer this.

Sex World

I live in Thailand, the proverbial "Land of Smiles". Thailand has half a million Thai men visiting sex workers *every day*; brothels the size of skyscrapers; clubs for women - gay and straight; stunning ladyboys; 7 out of 10 Thai males losing their virginity to a sex worker; a worldwide reputation as a 'gay paradise'; and Pattaya - probably the world's first purpose-built, sex-for-sale city.

Thailand certainly has a lot of smiling people, but it is also a country with a problem. No, not too much sex, but too many Western-imposed values. Prostitution is illegal in Thailand and yet there are millions of sex workers and millions more clients. How does that happen? Well, it happens because in 1960 Thailand succumbed to pressure from the U.N. to make prostitution illegal - Thailand wanted to be seen as 'equal' to the West in terms of its cultural and social values. However, this sop to Westernism made not a jot of difference to the Thai sex industry; indeed, during the past 50 years it has grown to the point that it now constitutes some 15% of Thailand's GDP.

Monogamy as a concept is well understood in Thailand it is just that not many Thai's bother to practice it.

And yet despite this prevalence of sex, Thai society survives. Indeed, it thrives; it is deeply spiritual, highly communal and family values are much stronger than in the West. How is this achieved? It is achieved by the Thai's virtually ignoring Western values while paying lip-service to them. Now you might say this is hypocritical, and I wouldn't argue that point. But the truth is most countries are hypocritical when it comes to sex, not least America and the UK. They just don't like admitting it.

Enforced monogamy is a mistake that people around the world are now trying to put right

It is obvious the Thai's don't intend to cease buying and selling sex. And nor do they intend to legalise prostitution. So, like the rest of the world they come to occupy a paradoxical space between social expectations and individual practice.

It is very likely you too live in such a space, or you have done at some point in your life. Truth is, most people do, no matter what their nationality. Which tells us that societal values are desperately out of synch with individual practice. Basically, we are not doing what we are preaching.

Our moralist conflict over sex is not new. Certainly it goes back to the 18th century in the West and was especially apparent in Victorian attitudes. But surely we have moved on from those days? Were not the 1960's supposed to free us up from the sexual hang-ups and inhibitions that tormented our parents and grandparents? Apparently not, for sexual hang-ups are not only still with us, in my view we are seeing the emergence of a revitalised conservatism in Western society when it comes to sex. We may be more comfortable with diversity in sexual identity, e.g. LGBT people (lesbian, gay, bi and transgendered), but we haven't moved on much when it comes to recognising that monogamy does not work for most of us. Moreover, that this wholesale insistence on monogamy being at the heart of 'love relationships' is, in truth, the main reason why most relationships breakdown. More evidence, if it were needed, that we are patently unable to adhere to the sexual codes that society and culture impose on us.

Alas, this hypocritical stance does not stop us adopting moralistic judgments towards those whom we consider to have sexually 'misbehaved'. Too many of us find the pulpit a comfortable place in which to stand.

When it comes to sexual pleasure, both youth and virginity are seriously over-rated

One of the most disturbing trends in recent years has been the almost ritualised public humiliation now heaped on those in the public eye who 'stray'. Politicians and sports stars are especially vulnerable to what appears to be an increasing desire in the West for condemnation of those who do not rigorously follow the 'monogamous code'. The media and all its attendant mouths feed on these 'sex scandals' like jackals at a carcass. Eventually, some shame-faced male politician will be forced to the cameras, most likely holding his grim-looking wife's hand, and confess; state his remorse, admit his shame and then resolve never to do it again. At this point the jackals seem satiated. They then go hunting for their next victim.

So as to avoid such a spectacle, - which actually has a lot in common with the ancient British tradition of putting miscreants in the village stocks and pelting them with rotten eggs - wealthy celebrities now attempt to get a 'super- injunction' thereby legally prohibiting the media from naming them in any 'sex scandal'. However, with social networking now firmly embedded in society, keeping oneself anonymous under such circumstances is, as many have discovered, highly problematic at least.

This baying public frenzy may be driven by the sad media circus but it reveals both a voyeurism and a sexual frustration at the heart of society. It signals an immaturity in us, as if despite living in the 21st century we are not yet fully grown up when it comes to sex and sexuality. There is a deep and ingrained conservative attitude and unease in the West about sex. As many social commentators have noted, the USA seems far more comfortable with violence than it does with sex and human sexuality. While the British love to follow the sexual scandals of celebrities even while behaving in a licentious way themselves.

Only in the USA could you find numerous 'sex therapists' - people who will 'counsel' you out of your supposed 'sex addiction'. Tiger Woods was not the first celebrity to put himself through this dubious process and for sure he won't be the last; the corporate sponsors hate the taint of sexual scandal. Again, this is just indicative of the fact we haven't fully accepted and come to terms with our innate sexuality. We seek sex but at the same time it triggers a deep disquiet in us, one which fuels the very voyeurism that, for example, not only makes porn now one of the biggest industries in the world, with one estimate claiming 28,000 people are watching internet porn *every second,* but, I suspect, also contributes to the increased incidence of child sex abuse.

Natural desire makes sex addicts of us all

That which we cannot avoid in ourselves and yet is condemned by society as 'wrong', so we feel compelled to hide. And it is in this act of hiding and concealing from others, and from ourselves, that lurk the psychological dangers. Those of us who are not having sufficient healthy sex with real-life adults find it all too easy to retreat to the solo-sex of computer porn and such like. At this point, sex becomes a desire we cannot wholly satisfy - even while we are confronted by it every day of our lives: sex is not only in our heads, it is physically all around us - in advertising, every aspect of the media, out on the streets; you can find it in the virtual worlds of second-life, and you can find it down some back-alley in your local town. Yet we can rarely bring ourselves to talk about it, let alone go out and have it in a free and mutual way, especially if we are in a 'monogamous' relationship. This triggers the voyeuristic, hypocritical obsession that, I suggest, bedevils the possibility of having honest and open relationships.

Not all countries succumb to this hypocritical stance over sex, at least not to the extent we now see in the US, the UK and other parts of northern Europe. Certainly Thailand and most of Asia does not, neither does Italy, France and pretty much all of South America. It appears to be very much an Anglo-Saxon disease. Nevertheless, as Westernisation spreads, so too does the disease.

One of the forces stopping the disease getting into the heart of Asian countries is the lack of guilt that Asian societies attach to sex in the first place.

One of the fundamental differences between the East and the West concerns the concepts of guilt and shame. As management theorist, Professor Nancy Adler, explains, in collectivist societies such as those of Southeast Asia and China, the social pressure on individuals is to maintain 'face'. That is, at all times ensure social harmony and do nothing to bring shame on oneself or one's family. These are societies built on communality; every member contributes, or is expected to. The concept of face is extremely powerful, as is the pressure to avoid shame - the public loss of face.

And across Asia, especially Southeast Asia, there has, historically, been no loss of face attached to sexual practice - so long as it is not done in such a way as to bring shame on the family or loved ones. Which is one of the main reasons why visiting a sex worker is seen not as shameful, but a natural outlet for sexual desire - both men's and women's. Sex may not be spoken about openly in the East, and Asian cultures penalise public expressions of sexuality, even overt affection, but individuals can have as much sex as they want, and with whom they want, so long as it is done behind closed doors.

Everyone pays for sex one way or another

The West is very different. There, the individualistic culture and social codes instil in us the concept of guilt. This is internalised, individualised guilt, whereby if we transgress some moral or legal code then we are expected to duly *feel guilty* about it. The East has no term for internalised guilt. It just doesn't translate. Most Asian's understand guilt as being in the wrong, being culpable, being found guilty in a court of law; they don't internalise guilt as a feeling that they should deal with through, for example, repentance and confession. Instead, they feel shame. At all times, the emphasis is on social harmony - communalism and ensuring harmony in the collective. In the West, the desire is to avoid 'feeling guilty' - individualism. The aim is the same in that both guilt and shame, in different ways, provide social sanction against those who transgress certain codes of behaviour. But the outcomes are very different indeed.

Hypocrisy is the stronghold of the fainthearted

In the East one can have sex outside marriage, just don't talk about it. In the West, one cannot have sex outside marriage under any circumstances - at least not without risking that insidious feeling of guilt.

In Jungian terms, two thousand years of Judeo-Christian religion have succeeded in instilling in the Western social subconscious copious and irresolvable feelings of guilt over sex and the pleasure it brings. And the more that sex surfaces in society, not least through the media and the Internet, so the more the West has to confront this paradoxical state.

One response is the compulsion to control it - most notably through the expectation that one will feel guilty if one sexually misbehaves; hence the very public hounding and humiliation of those who transgress, sexually. More formal methods of control are evident through the attempt to render the selling and/or paying for sex, illegal. This pressure to prohibit not just prostitution but also strip clubs and lap dancing, is being increasingly applied by governments and religious groups throughout the Western world.

The West is indeed, in state of voyeuristic Puritanism, which, just like the old Puritanism, cannot accept the fact that, in the final analysis, the world is a sexual place and people will act out their sexual needs, whatever.

Asia, on the other hand, has experienced over 2500 years of Buddhism and Hinduism; benign and sophisticated religions that recognise human desire, sexual and otherwise, as entirely normal indeed in some instances to be celebrated, just so long as social harmony is maintained.

Spicing it Up

Only the person who can satisfy their sexual needs without guilt or shame is truly free

Given the rampant hypocrisy that operates around sex worldwide it comes as no surprise to find the same hypocrisy operating in intimate relationships. Now it might be that maintaining a hypocritical and contradictory stance regards sex can hold a couple together. For example, both partners know that one or both cheat on each other they just don't declare it openly thereby avoiding confrontation. Many long-term relationships operate on precisely this arrangement. Is this wrong, morally? Not in my opinion, though it is sad in that it confirms the lack of honesty at the heart of such relationships. Rather than the relationship being founded on openness, it is founded on hypocrisy and secrets.

A contrasting arrangement is one I came across in Southeast Asia. In this marriage both partners went to sex clubs for extra-marital fun - that is, they each paid for sex with a sex worker. This arrangement operated two or three times a week. The husband took his wife to her club (where she had a regular liaison booked with younger males), after which he drove off to his club for likewise but with younger women. Several hours later, he picked up his wife and both drove back home, apparently satisfied, and happy.

All this couple are doing is dealing with the hard truth that virtually all sexual relationships become habitualised after about three to six years, depending on the circumstances of the relationship. And after a decade of having sex with the same person, most of us are tempted with something new. This does not necessarily mean there is the absence of love in the relationship, only an absence of sexual excitement. However, this sexual vacuum heralds the crunch moment for most relationships. How couples handle it determines their future together.

Habit and predictability equal boredom and nothing kills sexual desire as quickly as boredom, in which case it would seem logical to inject some unpredictability into the relationship so as to ensure the sexual spice continues. This is what the Southeast Asian couple were doing. Millions of other couples do something similar. It is called swinging, or partner swapping.

One of my own awakenings to the realities of human sex and sexuality came during my visits to swingers clubs in Europe and through meeting couples who were looking for sexual encounters with other couples in a free and open way. The Internet is really a potent medium for such people to meet and this has helped swinging or partner swapping growing phenomenally over the past two decades. It is estimated there are now approximately 500,000 couples (1 million people) in the UK alone who have 'swung'; that is, had sex with other couples or individuals as a social or leisure activity, sometimes in swinging clubs, or in hotels and houses. Research undertaken in Italy suggests some 700,000 Italians partner swap. Germany has the highest number of swingers clubs, though Japan, Britain and France are not far behind. Australia, South Africa and New Zealand have also seen a large increase in the number of swingers clubs and people using them. Though little research has been done into the number of heterosexual swingers, reliable estimates put it at between 3% and 10% of all couples in the West. Given there are approximately 77 million couples in the USA that would indicate at least 2.5 million couples, or 5 million swingers in that country alone. Seems Americans are not so puritanical as we thought.

Given the incidence of swinging it is clearly not 'abnormal'; indeed, it is a very normal activity for many people. My visits to swingers clubs in Oslo, Copenhagen, Austria and the UK, confirmed that most couples are middle class, educated and in committed relationships. They are of all ages and professional backgrounds. Their behaviour in clubs is very polite and follows quite strict rules of 'not touching unless invited'. Condoms are pretty much compulsory. Those who seek some 'privacy' in a club can find it, as can those who prefer more exhibition sex. Most clubs cater for bondage and mild S&M tastes, though this seems to be a minority activity. The clubs operate in a very welcoming and easy-going manner. Food and drink is usually on offer and couples are made to feel welcome, relaxed and comfortable. It is incredibly enlightening to see men and women naked and half-dressed, walking around casually, at ease and enjoying themselves sexually and in a totally non-judgmental environment.

Some couples do what is termed a 'soft swap' whereby there is no penetrative sex, just touching or perhaps oral. Others go to watch and have sex themselves, but not share. Many go for the full sex encounter with others. For lots of women, going to a swingers club also allows them to satisfy their bisexual feelings. Some couples prefer not to visit clubs and instead contact other couples initially anonymously online. I met such a couple in Oslo, both Danes, professionals in their late 40s, married with grown-up children. They never visited swingers clubs, preferring to contact other couples online, then meet for lunch or dinner, and if all seemed happy, proceed to a city hotel.

> *Swinging is the only socialist-utopian activity to have not only survived the 20th century but actually gotten more popular*

All couples clearly discuss and agree the particular codes and arrangement they intend to follow before they go to a club or meet other couples. I met one Norwegian couple where the wife engaged in sex with other men, but the husband only watched. That was their arrangement. A younger German couple I met were into very intricate rope bondage, though this was purely exhibitionist and for their pleasure only. They did not perform bondage on others nor allow others to perform bondage on them.

My own observations and encounters in swinging clubs and with couples who swap, supports that of author Ewan Morrison, who based his book *'Swung'* on his experiences as a swinger/researcher. As he confirms, being part of a swinging scene creates a "feeling of an almost-socialist utopia of open-mindedness and tolerance...there is a lot of laughter, friendship and love". That is certainly how I experienced it, and my partner at the time felt likewise. It was, indeed, an enlightening and fascinating experience for both of us, with the sex being simply engaged in for pleasure but the actual openness of the whole encounter producing feelings of togetherness, connection, even love.

And that is the interesting paradox, the fact that most of the couples who swing are in love with each other, very close, intimate and enjoying a full and balanced relationship. They seem happy. Indeed, all the research into swinging couples suggests they are very contented in their relationships. Which would make sense as couples not at ease with each other could not participate. I never once saw any couple argue or fall out in a club. There is an impressive absence of jealousy. Every couple I met were partaking openly and willingly. There was no coercion that I saw. There was a lot of pleasure and honesty.

Every orgasm is a moment of sweet death

So, is swinging strange? Only if you think that monogamy is normal and essential to the human condition. But then recent research published into the sexual habits of Stone Age humans strongly indicates that they too engaged in practices such as group sex, bondage, transvestism and used sex toys. As Professor Timothy Taylor, archaeologist at Bradford University states;

"The research into Stone Age human's sex lives shows that far from having intercourse simply to reproduce, they had sex for fun. It is clear that monogamy only became established as hunter-gather societies took up agriculture and settled in houses, allowing the social roles of men and women to become more fixed."

Dr Petra Boynton, a relationship counsellor and health lecturer at University College, London, considers this research 'refreshing". As she says; "so much evolutionary theory promotes the idea that humans, particularly women, are preprogrammed for monogamy, but that is often simply overlaying science on a preexisting view of society."

So it seems that modern relationships are hypocritical for a reason - they are built on two fundamental misconceptions; the first is that monogamy is normal for humans, and is indeed essential for happiness with another person; the second is that women are essentially monogamous and that men are the gender with the unbridled libido.

Once one has witnessed couples engaging in free and open sex with each other but under clearly defined conditions of mutual care and responsibility, then it truly removes the blinkers from one's eyes about human sexuality. As Ewan Morrison and others who have engaged in participative research into swinging have confirmed, we can learn much about society and about ourselves from being part of something so social and yet so intimate. Certainly I learned to appreciate the fundamental pleasure of sex and to embrace a more open and honest approach to it. As my awareness grew, so any guilt I might have had, disappeared. What began as research into my own sexuality became a most liberating experience; my self-awareness grew, my compassion for others deepened, as did my appreciation and acceptance of difference.

Once we place this apparently 'odd' sexual practice in an historical context, and realise that it is not odd at all but fundamentally human, then one can only conclude that monogamy is the problem, not the solution. Certainly, this is the conclusion of my visits, experiences, encounters and research into swinging, partner swapping, and sex work across all continents. Monogamy is a social invention. It is not natural. Few of us are practicing it, and even fewer of us want to. But how many of us are strong enough to admit we have a problem with monogamy? Not many. The codes of guilt and shame are too powerful.

Many people would like to swing they just don't want to get undressed in public

Example:

Dirk is 36. Petra is 33. They are Austrian and have been together for over twelve years. They first met at Hamburg University where both were studying law. They began living together at university and continued the relationship after graduation. They now live in Vienna where both have jobs in law. About four years ago they separated for a short while. Petra had a brief relationship with someone at work and she decided to leave Dirk. Despite having love for each other the sexual excitement had gone from their relationship. However, after a short time living as singletons, both realised they would rather be together than apart, so they gave it another go. Around this time a couple they were friendly with invited them to join them on a visit to a swingers club in the city. Dirk and Petra had never tried this activity before but felt it might enhance the sexual side of their relationship. Their first visit felt strange and they took time to acclimatise to the swinging culture. But they agreed to continue. Dirk and Petra enjoyed the feeling of sexual freedom and physical pleasure that came with swinging, and they were captivated by the relaxed and mature atmosphere of the clubs they visited. They now make it a rule never to visit swinging clubs singly, but only as a couple. They go three times a month. Sometimes they have sex with other individuals or couples, sometimes not. They have established rules of contact that work for them in these clubs and now tend to swing mostly with a small number of couples they have met. They feel their relationship is stronger and more stable, as a consequence of being much more sexually open.

Sex Myths

Sex is ultimately about pleasure - procreation is a secondary consequence we have to guard against

I am not seeking to promote swinging for everyone and nor am I suggesting that swinging is the solution to sexual boredom in all relationships; it might be for some couples, but for many others, probably not. Clearly, swinging is not a leisure activity suited to everyone. This type of activity will test a relationship - especially in the area of jealousy, inevitably in terms of an individual's moral code. What I am advocating is honesty and openness, and not being afraid to experiment.

But first we have to be honest and open with ourselves. How many of us engage in sex activities that might be perceived in a negative and judgmental light by others? How often have you rushed to condemn others for their sexual behaviour yet done something similar yourself? Now I am not talking here about illegal sex, but sex between consenting adults, especially infidelity. And, as we know, there are many avenues to infidelity.

Take the examples of sex work, including sex tourism. At its most unpleasant and nasty this includes child sex abuse, human trafficking, sex slavery and the sexual oppression of men, women and children for profit. No decent person could countenance any of these practices. But there are many millions of tourists who partake of sex with local people - adults - and pay them for doing so. Countries such as Indonesia, Thailand, China, India and the Philippines have well-established sex industries, probably earning these countries up to 15% of their GDP. Every city and town in the world has sex for sale and these sex workers mostly service local residents, not tourists. If you look for it, you can find it. This clearly tells us there is a need. And who are the buyers? Well they are people like you. They are not monsters.

Many are married or in relationships, some are lonely and in need of sexual satisfaction. All do it because it is pleasurable. To assume that any person who pays for sex with a sex worker or travels abroad and does so is immoral and bad, is not only a big mistake it is profoundly stupid. This attitude is not only harsh it is irrational as it would immediately condemn anyone who has ever paid for sex, or sold sex - certainly millions probably over a billion people.

Unlike men, who have physical limits, women are built to enjoy sex

So let us debunk the myth that sex work, and indeed sex tourism is always and inevitably bad. It is not. What is bad is child sex abuse and trafficking. Let us also debunk the myth that sex workers are simply prostitutes. They are not. It is important to distinguish sex work from prostitution. I define prostitution as an overarching term that encompasses every aspect of selling sex - including child sex, trafficking, sex slavery and the like. Sex work, by contrast, is just that - paid work undertaken by adults through choice.

I know many Westerners reading this will find it hard to appreciate that anyone, man or woman, could undertake sex work out of choice, but that is because they haven't fully understood what is going on in this relationship between client and sex worker. They have become too blinkered by the moralistic judgments of society. For many sex workers their biggest problem is not the work, but the negative judgment that others have of them, plus the low status which society puts them in. Go to www.empowerfoundation.org and www.mplusthailand.com to learn more about sex workers and their striving for respect. Sure, you will see that money drives it, but so it drives all industries. At the same time, millions of sex workers also enjoy the social environment of their profession - these are often strong communities in their own right.

We all realise that sex work would disappear overnight if there were no customers willing to pay. But who are these customers? Well in the past it was almost exclusively men, gay and straight, but nowadays women too are the clients. Around the world, from Africa to South America, Southern Europe to Southeast Asia, women tourists are paying for sex with local men. What started out many years ago in countries like Gambia and Jamaica as the practice of a small number of older, Western women tourists has, through international travel and changes in the sexual behaviour of modern women, become a global phenomenon.

Some researchers consider that this increasing incidence of sex tourism, both by men and women, reflects relationship problems seen to exist now between the sexes back in their home countries. I disagree. The problems have always been there - loneliness, lack of empathy between partners, sexual boredom, lack of passion, and sheer curiosity about one's sexual potential but little opportunity to explore it. Sometimes people just want sex with someone different - and without any emotional complications - totally natural.

What sex tourism by women does prove is that they are just like men when it comes to desiring sex. They too can have great sex outside of a relationship. They too can be instrumental about sex, decide what they want from a sexual encounter, and if need be, go out and find it.

The notion that women can only enjoy sex when it comes with love is like saying women can only enjoy food if they are dining a la carte

Example:

Liz, Jane and Maggie are in their late 40s. They live in the UK. The three have been friends for many years. All three are divorced and had many relationships with men over the years, though they are each currently without a regular partner. They first met on holiday in Spain, over 20 years ago. At that time Liz was married, Jane and Maggie were divorcees. Liz's marriage also ended some years later. Around nine years ago the three started dating men they'd met online. They each went in and out of a number of relationships and while they didn't find the love commitment they were seeking, they did have a lot of fun. Six years ago they decided to go on holiday together. They chose Gambia, mainly because it was inexpensive, exotic, sunny and hot. None of them had been to Africa before and the holiday did not disappoint them. They found the country and the people really welcoming. And they enjoyed the company of the many good-looking young Gambian men who were only too willing to be their casual 'boyfriends' for a couple of weeks. Since then, Liz, Jane and Maggie have not only gone back to Gambia several times, but also travelled to the Caribbean. There they find a similar opportunity for sun, sand and sexual pleasure with handsome young local males. The three women do these holidays together once or twice a year. They are now very close, closer even than sisters. They look out for each other when on holiday and share their secret encounters. Each hopes to meet that 'special man' sometime in the future, but right now life is good and they are enjoying it to the full.

Sex is natural, but then so is walking - both are skills that need to be learned

Polyamory

Don't fancy the anonymous communal sex associated with swinging? Feel that paying for sex is ethically and morally wrong? Are attracted to people outside your relationship but just couldn't cope with the feelings of guilt which would accompany the cheating and the deceit? Then you have one option left, and that is polyamory.

Polyamory relationships are open, multiple and consensual. They are based on truth and honesty and acceptance of the possibility or reality of loving more than one person, or desiring more than one person. This is not polygamy; where a person has more than one wife or husband, but rather polyamory describes a situation where one or both partners have intimate and romantic encounters and relationships with others. These relationships may or may not have a sexual component, but that is a possibility.

The essence of polyamorous relationships is that they are open and consensual. Both partners accept that each can engage in more than one loving and sexual relationship and with the full knowledge and consent of the other. Whether these sexual engagements are emotionally fulfilling or merely casual, is an issue that the couple can negotiate for themselves. Some polyamorous couples might agree that casual sex with others is an acceptable part of their relationship or they may decide that the sex be limited to identified and known others, perhaps within a network of polyamorous friends and couples. At one end of the polyamorous spectrum you have couples who have negotiated a flexibility and openness within their sexual contract which might include casual encounters with anonymous others, and at the other end there are polyamorous families consisting a number of specific individuals who practice multiple sexual relationships with each other and who do so within the fabric of a loving, intimate relationship.

Polyamory is a relatively recent term but it is becoming increasingly mainstream in relationship discourse. In fact, the word itself first figured in the 2006 edition of the Oxford

Dictionary. Now there are groups of polyamorous couples not only in the USA (where one estimate puts the number at 500,000 couples) but also Europe and many other parts of the world (www.polyamory.com).

The strength of the polyamorous approach is that it is ethical. Indeed, it is described as ethical non-monogamy. The point being that it is underpinned by honesty and openness. So this is not cheating. It is not being deceitful. It is not lying.

Polyamory is, in my opinion, the future of many relationships, especially in the age of globalisation and the internet. Polyamorous relationships confirm the age-less truth which is that it is not sex itself which kills a relationship, but the breakdown of the trust contract between a couple when one of them cheats.

The first question anyone should ask of a new partner is "are you a mono or a poly?" The two sexual types are fundamentally incompatible.

Example:

Tim is 33, an architect living in Seattle, and part of a polyamorous cluster. This cluster consists of four individuals; one other man and two women. They are all in their 30s, they are all professionals living in Seattle. Tim's primary relationship is with Laura, and they have now been living together for eight years. Three years ago, Laura and Tim met Jenny through his work. With the agreement of all three, Jenny began a relationship with Tim, and this coincided with Jenny also starting a relationship with the fourth member, Mike. Now the four of them regularly meet up at weekends and see each other as respective couples. So Tim and Mike both, at different times, have sex with Laura and Jenny. The polyamorous relationship that they have evolved does not allow for group sex between the four of them, and the main committed relationship is between Tim and Laura. Simiilarly, should Jenny and Mike decide to have sex with any other person, outside the cluster, then they are free to do so. None of the people in this polyamorous cluster are bisexual, so the sex remains between the men and the women. Complicated? Yes. But it works for these individuals. As Laura puts it "I now know that what we and Tim have negotiated is a polyamorous contract. It means we do not cheat on each other, and it forces us to confront and deal with any feelings of jealousy or possession. I have a strong sex drive and while I do not love Mike, I am physically attracted to him, just as I am to Tim. I know this sort of arrangement would not suit everyone, but it certainly suits us and we are very happy with it."

Sex and Age

To enjoy sex to its fullest one needs lots of imagination and few inhibitions

Anybody who has ever had sex, alone or with someone else, has had to deal with feelings of guilt and shame. It takes years of practice to be able to have sex with different people and always without being encumbered by that heavy baggage of guilt. Most of us never reach that state, which is one reason why we end up being on our own - we just cannot bring ourselves to enjoy our bodies, and that of another, without feeling bad inside.

To have good, enjoyable and guilt-free sex with another person we need confidence in ourselves and in our bodies. We need to be able to let go and enjoy our full sexual and erotic potential as individuals. And this is one of the unrecognised aspects to sex - it is not only about pleasure but also about personal validation. By that I mean we engage with sex in order to be confirmed in our very identity as a man or woman. Sex really has the power to confirm our adult identity, which is one reason why young people engage in it so readily - not only because they are curious and may have some sexual desire, but because they see sex as a rite of passage that they need to go through in order to be seen and accepted as an 'adult' by their peers especially.

This sexual 'rite of passage' is not limited to teenagers - it can arise at any time in our lives. And when it does it often comes with issues around age attached to it.

Society still gets troubled by the thought of people of vastly different ages having sex together; this is perfectly understandable when it comes to under-age sex, but not so understandable when it comes to sex between consenting adults. Women in their 50s or 60s having sex with men in their 20s - what is wrong with that? Nothing. Men in their 50s or 60s having sex with women in their 20s - what is wrong with that? Nothing.

So long as the sex is consensual then people should not be judgemental. Alas, people too often are; they feel unsettled and confused. What society needs to appreciate is this issue of identity validation. For an older woman, having sex with a younger man is not only potentially very pleasurable and satisfying, the very fact of the younger man being aroused and satisfied gives the woman a powerful sense of being validated as a female and at a time in her life when she may feel especially vulnerable to her changing body and, consequently, self-image as a sexual being. The same drive is often the reason why younger women are attracted to older men and visa versa. The older man, if he is attractive, confident and considerate, can provide a really strong gender validation of the younger woman through the sexual relationship. Likewise, the older man feels his own sense of masculinity being strengthened. It is more than simply sexual desire, it is what emotional and identity validation each partner brings the other. In short, those sexual relationships that have a big age gap are the ones with the capacity to really strengthen not only our confidence but to reinforce our very sense of gender, sexuality, self-worth and identity. We should not deny these relationships to others, nor to ourselves.

Example:

Amina is a 25 year old Kenyan woman. She comes from a wealthy family who live in Nairobi. When she was 19, Amina went to the USA to do a degree in politics and law. During her final year at university Amina had an affair with one of her professors. He was aged 60. This professor was a famous academic who was known for being very open about his sexuality and easy-going lifestyle. Amina, now looking back on that relationship, describes it in this way: "I was not attracted to him at first, this grew as I got to know him as a person. We went out initially with other students as a group, but then he and I started seeing each other just the two of us. It began as a friendship. We connected. The sex was not necessary, but without it I felt something would have been missing. So it was as much at my instigation as his. At first I couldn't believe I was attracted to someone his age. He is not unattractive, but it was his respect for me as a woman and emotional maturity that I needed. He is an emotionally open man, and not many men are like that. I have not been able to tell many people about this relationship because I know they'll not understand and be judgmental. But I understand and that is what is important. I am so glad I had the relationship with my professor. It was thrilling, satisfying and I learned a lot about myself as a woman. He understands women and he treated me like an adult woman, an equal, and with total respect. In a way, he has spoiled me for other men because I now set my standards high when it comes to potential lovers. But that relationship with my professor was one of the best things to have happened in my life so far. It empowered me so much. We are still friends and stay in touch."

Something Amiss

Good sex is when the mind and body are in perfect harmony

I have sometimes been asked, "what sort of world do you think you are creating by your promotion of such an open and liberal attitude towards sexuality?"

My answer to this question is simply that sociologists like myself do not 'create' or 'invent' the world, we do not and cannot create reality. We just research it and then report on our findings. At the same time, we are human too. We have our opinions, judgments and political positions. So we are never entirely neutral. But we do try and achieve balance. We are not journalists seeking a sensational 'scoop' every other weekend and at whatever cost to the 'truth'. We are professionals interested in exploring society and identity and very curious to discover how people are behaving, and why.

And this is my position regards monogamy; I do not have to denounce it, people are doing that for themselves through their everyday practices, especially those who are into polyamorous relationships. I merely conclude that monogamy is a falsehood for the simple reason that most people, self-evidently, cannot adhere to it, at least not for very long. The very few who can do so prove the rule - monogamy does not work for most of us, and certainly not as a lifetime condition.

The evidence for this claim is all around us. Like you, I have met very few people, women or men, who have only ever had sex with one person throughout their life. Pretty much every adult that I know has had more than one relationship, countless numbers of adults I know have had countless numbers of relationships. I have also met many who will have sexual encounters outside their relationship if certain conditions operate: e.g. the sex is available; there is little or no chance of their partner finding out. This is sex simply for pleasure, not a search for love.

Clearly there is something amiss given the overwhelming evidence that more and more of us are serial monogamists; polyamorous, paying for sex; swinging and swapping; having a succession of sexual partners; using the internet to find sex; and playing away if the opportunity presents itself.

The clitoris is the only part of the human anatomy designed exclusively for pleasure

What is amiss is not the prevalence of sexual activity around the world; was it ever thus? The problem is that we don't want to face up to this reality. We would rather keep it hidden, silence it, and render it invisible; many of us preferring to retreat to our ideological comfort zones and pontificate from the sidelines. Unfortunately, 21st century sex reality refuses to go away - it is all around us. Just look at your own life and lives of those around you if you doubt me.

Just like marriage, so the monogamous code has broken down. It didn't take much. A few decades of industrial and economic prosperity, coupled with the opening up of the world through globalisation, and the idea of 'sex with one partner for the rest of one's life', lies in tatters.

As I say, I didn't break the code. I am just telling you it is broken.

But once we can rid ourselves of the ideological chains that would condemn sexual pleasure with many people, accept our sexual needs and identities, and not expect monogamy from every relationship we are in, or from ourselves, then so we can move on and to a much healthier place.

It is the lies, deceit, hypocrisy, manipulation and breakdown of trust that kills relationships. This is the true cancer at work in the relationship body. The sex is merely the vehicle from which this cancer invariably emerges. But it need not be - we can remove it from the equation and be much happier as a consequence, and undoubtedly stronger in our relationships.

Vagina liberation is the inevitable and welcome result of 100 years of feminism

I am encouraged by the awesome growth in women's self-awareness and sexual confidence. Feminist author, Germaine Greer, was one of those women who signalled this change back in the 1970s, though it took another 30 years for it to really permeate through most women's subconscious. What one might call 'vagina liberation' is now a worldwide phenomenon. Vagina liberation is women understanding their bodies, taking control of their sexuality, exploring their possibilities for sexual pleasure, embracing the joy of female sex without guilt or shame, and recognising that being a woman does not preclude a strong sexual identity and expressiveness. These are all positives and most welcome. The change in women's sexuality, at least the more open expression of it, is quite recent so it is still quite fragile. But given its worldwide dimensions it is unlikely to disappear soon, indeed it can only get stronger.

Younger women especially are more open and sexually aware. They appear unattached to the condition of virginity and eager to explore their sexual identities with numerous people - both male and female. While more and more older women, say those in their 50s and 60s, are enjoying the freedoms and pleasures which come from being liberated from those sex codes which inhibited their mother's possibility of sexual emancipation.

THE RELATIONSHIP MANIFESTO

This is how millions of women are living today around the world.

None of this precludes the possibility of a committed relationship with one partner at some point in the future for those women who are now single and sexually active, it just means they must accept that if they do promise fidelity then such a promise comes with risks. And to always be wary of any partner, man or woman, who promises the same, even if they promise it with good heart and sincerity.

Gay Sex

Real men can kiss each other on the lips

One of the most liberating and illuminative aspects of human sexuality concerns gay sex, both men to men and women to women. Same-sex relationships and encounters are especially empowering for society because they clearly signal that heterosexuality is not normal. Why? Because when it comes to sex, there is no normal. We have to discard the very idea of 'normal sex'; it is just another myth that binds.

Well, you might counter by saying that heterosexuality is the more common type of sexual identity and male-female sex the more common sexual practice. And I would agree. But being more common doesn't make it normal. Ants and fleas are more common than lions and tigers, but does that then make lions and tigers 'unnatural'? Obviously not.

Some anti-gay activists claim that gay sex is unnatural because it doesn't lead to procreation. My answer to that is that my sex life has not led to procreation since I had a vasectomy back in 1999. Maybe we should exercise a sex ban on anyone who cannot have children. That would be interesting. Similarly, what about all those women who enjoy regular sex but have gone through the menopause? Should we discriminate against them because they can no longer conceive?

The fact is, despite medical biologists spending decades trying to find the 'cause' of homosexuality, it cannot be found. Indeed, science cannot even produce a working hypothesis of what homosexuality actually is - it means different practices and different feelings to different people. We are left with recognising homosexuality as a complex but fundamental part of the human condition and therefore completely natural. Some people are attracted to members of the same sex and some are not. So it has always been. Professor Louis Gooren, Dutch expert on the biological characteristics of homosexuality and transsexuality, concludes that gay and lesbian sexuality connects in complex ways to both our biology and social environment. We each carry an individualised 'love map' in our minds one which contains not only sexual and erotic imagery that we find arousing, but also captures the notion of our idealized lover. As Professor Gooren confirms, ultimately we come down to the unfathomable variations at the heart of the human condition.

Example:

Marianne is aged 60. She is French but now lives in Vietnam. Marianne was born Maurice, a male. When he was 23, Maurice got married and over the next eighteen had two children. He had a successful career as a director with the French Airport Authority. Then his wife died of cancer at the age of 39. For a number of years Maurice lived alone, rarely socialising. However, this period encouraged him to reconsider his life, in particular his very identity as a man. Despite being married, Maurice had always had strong feelings of femininity and these intensified during his 40s, until, at the age of 49, he decided to change his sex. Maurice had to then undergo extensive medical and psychiatric evaluations because up until 2010, France still considered transsexuality to be a mental illness. However, he was subsequently given approval to undergo full gender reassignment surgery e.g. have his penis removed and a vagina created, and this he did aged 56. Following this surgery, Maurice was legally designated as a woman, changed her legal identity including passport, and became Marianne. Although Marianne had received full support from her employers during this period, she decided to take early retirement and live in Southeast Asia. She eventually settled in Ho Chi Minh City where she met Took. Took is female, aged 36. Maurice and Took now live together as a lesbian couple. They are very much in love.

What people do, sexually, in privacy and consensually should not concern society so long as minors are not involved. But we should be interested in the sexual variety that exists around us, because this is both illuminating and instructive as to the reality at the heart of the human condition. As research shows, humans have been into same sex, bondage, group sex, sex for material reward, and sadomasochism since they first came down from the trees. There is nothing new under the sun when it comes to sex - though still we try and deny it.

One reason for this depressing state of denial over sex is that as societies became more organised and structured around dominant religious codes and middle class values, so sex became infused with the notion of 'compulsory heterosexuality'. That is, heterosexuality, as practice and identity, becomes the paradigm, the natural, the norm, the privileged. Out of this emerge legal and moral restrictions not only around gay sex and homosexual identities, but any sexual practices regarded as 'unnatural' by those who place themselves as moral overseers of the rest of us. This can lead to the bizarre and depressing situation that allows seven states in the USA to still have legislation on their books that makes sodomy (classified as both anal and oral sex) a felony. The eighth state was Louisiana, until July 2011 when that state finally booted its law of 'solicitation of crimes against nature' out the back door. Now Louisianan's can use the back door as much as they like without risk of ending up in jail.

But though Louisiana finally moves itself into the 20th century, there remain 85 countries where consensual same-sex acts between adults are criminalized. These include so-called 'developed' nations such as Singapore and Malaysia. In 190 countries gay marriage is banned, and 7 countries have the death penalty for gay sex, one of which is Saudi Arabia.

We do not know if the human race is fundamentally bisexual, but it's certainly worth finding out

Variety signals difference and diversity is all around us, indeed it is fundamental to the human condition. Attempting to create social hierarchies of privilege and oppression based on difference is when the problems start. Ignorance and lack of human empathy breed arrogance in those who come to consider themselves 'normal' and 'superior'. Which leads to a situation where gays can be 'legally' imprisoned or executed for being gay.

But what is the problem with being gay? For many who consider themselves 'straight', the problem would appear to be the very idea of gay sex - e.g. men performing anal sex and oral sex on each other. (straight men have fewer hang-ups over lesbian sex) But why condemn this? Straight men are only too happy to have a woman perform oral sex on them, while most women enjoy cunnilingus. Similarly, anal sex is a pleasure that millions of straight men enjoy and a lot of straight women seek in their relationships also. The hypocritical stance is breathtaking.

At its most ridiculous we arrive at a situation whereby men have to go around performing outlandish and ridiculous roles of macho straight masculinity so as to be seen as 'proper men'. The very contradictions inherent in this performance get exposed not least when men are imprisoned. What happens in male prisons? Men have sex with each other - all those straight 'macho' guys apparently no longer hung-up about gay sex. As Tony Soprano explained in one episode of the Sopranos television series, "men get a pass for this".

What is it that attracts us to others? Even this is not clear. Gay men appear to be attracted to masculine performance while straight men appear to be attracted to feminine performance. But then there are gay men who can have sex with masculine women (lesbians) and millions of straight men have sex with ladyboys (transsexuals). The bars and clubs of South America and Southeast Asia especially are full of transsexuals who have sex with 'straight' men. Indeed, I know many otherwise straight men that have had sex with Thai ladyboys (women with penises) and enjoyed it immensely.

This is why gay sex is so important to the human condition. Every time a gay man has anal sex with another man, a lesbian woman goes down on her female lover, or a straight man gets fellated by a ladyboy, then the assumption of 'normal heterosexuality', indeed the very idea of a gender binary, gets, as feminist sociologist Professor Judith Butler puts it, 'troubled' and unsettled. And it is in this troubling that we can free ourselves from those social, legal and cultural codes that would otherwise seek to define our identities, limit our potential, burden us with guilt and shame, reduce our opportunity for sexual pleasure, and negatively judge those who do not adhere to compulsory heterosexuality.

Many of my male friends are gay. In fact, overall, I prefer the company of gay men to straight men. Why is that? Well, it is not because I am gay; actually I am straight but 'playful'. No, it is because I find gay men mostly open, candid and revealing about their sexual identities and their relationships. Get a group of gay men and women (of whatever sexuality) together and the conversation is fascinating, lively and expressive. One can go for hours without ever mentioning sport, fast cars, computer games, the latest i-product, or how pissed one got the night before. Gay men learn to be reflective as most women do. This reflexivity of the self provides the basis for a more open, informed and empathetic social interaction plus a distinct lack of strident masculine competitiveness between the males.

One thing that gay men do like to talk about is their sexual relationships. Which is very different to most straight men who are either totally unable to talk about sexual relationships in any way whatsoever, or do so only through the context of conquest. And I know there are exceptions to this rule, but for many men, detailed talk about the self in terms of their masculinity, the intimate and the sexual and how they feel about these aspects of their being, remains a no-go area.

This dominant discourse of sex and relationships which gay men engage in might seem to confirm the idea that gay men are promiscuous. Well I think not. Gay men are no different to straight men - they are just more open and honest about what they do, what they like and what they are looking for. This is so refreshing. What is also refreshing is that the very concept of 'promiscuity' does not work within gay and lesbian sexual culture, at least not from what I have seen. I have long realised that one word which requires removing altogether from the English language is 'promiscuous'. It is so pejorative. We can live perfectly well without it. Promiscuity only makes sense if we can define a universal moral code that unambiguously defines 'normal' in respect of sexual practice. Not a chance.

We need to redefine marriage in order to save it

Gay men and lesbians contain most of the world's true sexual radicals. They are the one's who challenge us all to re-evaluate, reconsider and redefine our assumptions as to what is ' normal' not only in terms of sex, but also in terms of relationships.

This is especially apparent now in the number of same-sex marriages that are sexually open. Recently published research by Coleen Hoff, Clinical Psychologist and Professor of Sexuality Studies at San Francisco State University, reveals that for many gay marriages, monogamy is not a central feature of the relationship. Hoff followed 556 male couples for three years and found that 50% have sex outside of their relationships, with the knowledge and approval of their partners. As Hoff says; "Consent is the key. With straight people it is called affairs or cheating, but with gay people it does not have such negative connotations".

The study also found that gay couples are not only very happy in their open relationships but that these relationships tend to last. A different study, published in 1985, also concluded that open gay relationships lasted longer. It is the transparency and the honesty, freedom and mutual understanding that strengthens the relationship and thereby reduces the risk of the 'trust contract' being broken.

The open gay relationship is fundamentally no different to the open straight one. Increasing numbers of both gay and straight couples, around the world, are now creating their own unique polyamorous relationships and which have the fundamental characteristic of being consensual and open. The word 'cheating' is removed from the relationship vocabulary and replaced with honesty.

Around the world, the traditional marriage is in crisis. We need change, we need insight, and we need honesty and openness if marriage is to survive at all. Without it, marriage is finished;

it will be reduced to being no more than a rite of passage that a decreasing number of women feel they must go through in order to validate their adult femininity. That is where marriage is heading today. The innovations spearheaded by polyamorous couples, both gay and straight, might save it.

But first we need to encourage people to ditch the old myth which states that monogamy is the 'only way to live in a stable and committed relationship', and secondly to encourage people to wake up to the reality and diversity of 21st century love and relationships.

We are then left with the issue of how to bring openness into a marriage or any committed relationship. As with gay and lesbian couples in open relationships, straight open relationships require mutuality and agreement first. This is fundamental otherwise they won't survive. The partners need to be honest about encounters, maybe seek advance approval of partners, and have no secrecy between them. Couples need rules - but they can construct these rules for themselves, they do not need society to do it for them. This is what being in a 21st century committed relationship entails - being mature and open enough to recognise one's needs and to build agreement and consensus about meeting these needs together as a couple and in a calm, informed and mutual way. This, in my opinion, is the only way keep people together.

Saying "I do' is not enough - Sacred vows will no longer keep you together after all else fails

Example:

Olivia and Emma are both aged 31. They are Australian and live in Sydney. Olivia works part-time and is studying for a PhD. Emma is a published author. They met six years ago at a party and have been

148

together pretty much every day since. They live in a rented house located just outside the city and in 2010 they got married. Their relationship has evolved to become not just close but open. Olivia has had relationships with men on occasion, though Emma has not. Emma has lived an exclusively lesbian identity all her adult life, while Olivia considers herself more bisexual. The decision to get married was not a hard one. They are in love and totally devoted to each other. Neither could envisage being in a relationship with anyone else. At the same time, they do have slightly different sexual needs and they have had to recognise this in order for their marriage to be strong and stable. Before they got married they contracted to keep their relationship open but honest. They consented to having occasional sex with others but only on the condition that they asked permission from each other before doing so. This contract has been operative for four years and is fundamental to their marriage vows. One aspect of their relationship contract is that they agree never to spend a night apart unless absolutely unavoidable, and never to spend a night with anyone else. The contract they have devised works for them and they know many same-sex couples with similar arrangements. They have not so far been able to reveal the contract to their respective families. In time, Olivia and Emma are hoping to adopt a child. For them, being together is for life. They long ago stopped confusing sex with love.

Being Honest

Sex bedevils us, makes us fearful of our passions and desires, and renders us emotionally vulnerable. It comes laden with guilt, shame and anxiety. It is, arguably, the most powerful natural force within humanity and yet one which none of us can entirely control, no matter our character, strength of mind or determination. But while sex unsettles and confuses us who would want to live a life without it? Not many. It is the most wonderful of pleasures, indeed, as *The Doors* lead singer, Jim Morrison, put it:

> **"When sex involves all the senses intensely, it can be like a mystical experience".**

Every intimate relationship offers the promise of this mystical experience, and in our hearts we know this; indeed it is something we seek with a partner. Which is why I believe sex and sexual pleasure are so fundamental to a relationship. To be sure we can have fulfilling relationships without sex, but they lack that crucial, intense and open physical intimacy which we all yearn for; in our sex life with a loved one so we can become fully released from the travails of daily life. Even sex without love can be delightfully exciting and satisfying. In fact, often sex without love feels the most unencumbered by expectation and routine. We should not deny ourselves this pleasure.

I believe the only way to fully enjoy sex and embrace our sexual identity, is to come to terms with it. This is why I have presented in this chapter aspects of sexuality and sexual practice that will not be common, or indeed acceptable, to all people. The aim is not to promote, for example, swinging or sex tourism as the only ways of achieving sexual pleasure, but to highlight the diversity around us, and to encourage people to accept this diversity without recrimination, judgment or guilt. It is up to the individual whether or not they wish to embrace it in their own lives. These are choices only we can make and no one should make for us.

You cannot be wholly free in your sex life unless you are open to alternative ways of being sexual, even if they are not for you. And being free in oneself, sexually, is important; it is vital to our growth as adults. As we change so too will our sexual desire, our sex needs, our erotic imagery, and the importance we attach to sex. For some of us, sex may get less important as we age, for others it becomes more important - an indicator of our ability to delay mortality and, at the very least, a wonderful way to relax.

I am well aware that many, if not most, people reading this book will be uncomfortable with being in a relationship that is not monogamous. Again, that is the choice of each individual. However, most of us are not monogamous, at least throughout our lives. We do monogamy at different times and with different people. Monogamy is an aspiration it is not a fixed attainable state that we can all adhere to with one person for the rest of our lives. So recognising this can help us accept our needs, and be honest not only with ourselves, but with our partners.

Most men know and accept that monogamy is an illusion; a state of being which exists only in social convention, not in practice - they accept this reality amongst themselves. It is one of the 'truths' that men understand and share with each other. Men together will very often reveal the extent of their 'playing', even if they have a tendency to exaggerate. The secrets that straight men are prepared to share amongst themselves, in terms of their infidelities, are many. A married man will tell even a casual male acquaintance that he has a secret lover, but he would never tell his wife - his soulmate, or probably another woman. Men share a lot in this respect. It is one of the areas in which men, both gay and straight, bond.

Most women can never be included into this secret reality of the male world - unless, of course, they are the party who is involved. They remain excluded forever by virtue of being women and therefore considered untrustworthy by men when it comes to male sex secrets. But then women keep their own secrets, infidelities and desires, that they would never share with a male partner or friend, but which they will often willingly reveal to a close female friend.

It is in this crucial area of secret lives that the worlds of the female and male become separated, and where relationships invariably come to grief.

So often we see relationships existing in this land of half-truth, myth, illusion, deception, and lies. On the surface, the relationship appears 'ok'. It may be long-lasting, committed, and built around a strong family lifestyle. But at its core are secrets that never get revealed, never get exposed, and never get spoken of.

What sort of love is it if we cannot talk to our loved one about one of the most important and fundamental aspects of our very being, our very identity? How strong and secure is a relationship built on lies and deception? For me, these are not full relationships - they are accommodations, largely functional and for social appearance only. They work very well at that level, but they operate fundamentally on pretence.

For me, the really strong relationships are where both parties have recognised and accepted their particular sex needs and consented to address them honestly and openly. Couples who swing must do this otherwise the relationship cannot survive. So must the millions of couples around the world that consent to one or both partners occasionally paying for sex. Most would consider this far healthier for the relationship than having a secret, regular lover. And openness and consent must be at the heart of those gay, lesbian and straight marriages that are increasingly factoring in a non-monogamous clause. These couples are preparing to meet the really big relationship challenge - sexual infidelity - head-on, not relying on hope, vows and expressions of love to keep it all together.

Really, it is easy to say 'I do'; it is easy to say 'I love you'; it is easy to say 'I will always be faithful'; and it is easy to say 'I will never want anyone else'. What is hard is being honest and accepting honesty from one's partner.

The truth can hurt, but it's the loss of trust that kills the relationship

Chapter 6: Togetherness

"A dream you dream alone is only a dream, a dream you dream together is reality" (John Lennon)

Whatever the particular dynamics of a relationship, all are ultimately about togetherness. For some couples this can mean weeks, sometimes months apart, perhaps communicating only by email or phone. For others it is based on never being apart for a single night or day. There is no one right way. It is for each couple to discover what best suits them. At the same time, however a couple define togetherness it always needs to be worked at - it will not come without understanding and agreement. Togetherness brings intimacy, warmth, comfort, validation and companionship, it also brings challenges and friction, and we should be prepared for this from the outset. In fact, friction is fundamental to any relationship - it is the dynamic, the grit if you like that gives the relationship some of its unique character and energy. Therefore, we should not be unduly concerned with friction rather we should be concerned with how we address it as a couple. In the final reckoning, friction is not the problem - what brings problems is not being able handle friction in a productive and consensual way.

In this chapter I am going to explore 13 primary aspects of togetherness and offer both particular philosophical/mental approaches - ways of looking at and being in relationships - together with some practical suggestions. Some of these practical suggestions might appear quite radical and will certainly challenge many people's assumptions about marriage especially. However, every suggestion is designed to achieve the following aims:

1. For couples to be together longer and happier

2. For singletons to be better prepared for relationships when they come along

Good togetherness is a state of mind, a willingness to listen and compromise, value and respect. It is a ongoing accommodation of the ego

1. Renewable Vows

I believe that relationship vows are powerful and significant ways of validating togetherness. It has become too easy for couples to join together and then split up when times get tough. There is a lightness to modern relationships that is unhealthy - it symbolises a lack of commitment and intensity. Too many of us are butterflies, flitting from one relationship to the next, not sticking around long enough to see it through to its optimum conclusion. At the same, marriage is currently too restricting, too limiting, brings with it unrealistic and unattainable expectations, and is far too demanding, sexually, financially and legally. As I have said, we need to reinvent it if it is to survive this coming century.

The purpose of the vow need not necessarily be to state one's commitment in the 'eyes of God', but merely to confirm a love and commitment to each other, publicly if necessary. I believe all couples that live together should do this. In the final chapter I give some examples of the sorts of vows that can be sworn by couples, depending on whether they are seeking to affirm their togetherness as part of a marriage ceremony or not.

At the same time, we need to recognize that ten years is at the very edge of time limits for the vast majority of relationships. Most are not sustainable beyond this period, marriages included.

Indeed, seven years is far more realistic. Therefore, I realise only too well that vows alone will not keep people together. Other elements need to be factored in.

So the practical suggestions offered below are based on these two fundamentals; the need for vows and the fact that ten years is a lifetime for most relationships.

1. *The Togetherness Vow: All couples commit to making a sworn vow to each other, preferably after about six months into the relationship.* This is not only for those couples who are living together, but any couple who feels ready and able to make a commitment with each other. The first six months is the testing period in any relationship - this is the phase when you'll decide whether it is worth making a commitment or not, and what is likely to be involved should you do so. It takes you beyond the 'honeymoon' weeks and into the realities of being together.

So avoid making any commitment during this first phase. Do so only after six months has passed. And both of you need to agree this. One person should not be putting pressure on the other to take the vow. This is not a marriage vow, it is a vow you make to each other either privately or with your friends and family. It carries no legal weight, only a duty of care and commitment that you willingly swear together. Examples of such vows are given in the final chapter. In my opinion, all couples should do this, whether they are intending to eventually get married or not.

2. *The Ten-Year Break-point: Vows must be renewed every ten years or the relationship is discontinued.* This is for all couples that take the 'togetherness vow', However, I believe that it should be applied to marriage vows also. My recommendation is that no marriage should legally be able to continue longer than ten years without both partners renewing their vows together. If one or both partners choose not to renew their vow then the marriage is over. No divorce, just each party legally going their separate

ways at that point. As I stress, this suggestion is applicable to all relationships. So, for example, those couples that have stayed together but never married, they too must renew their togetherness vow at the ten-year point. And every ten years that a couple are together, so they must renew their vow or the relationship comes to its natural conclusion.

This suggestion is radical but is designed to keep people together, not encourage them to split up. If taken up it will bring about a dramatic reduction in the number of divorces and enhance the togetherness possibilities of all committed relationships. It will also very likely encourage more people to get married. At the very least it will force individuals and couples to recognize that they cannot automatically assume longevity in a relationship - it needs to be worked at if it is to survive. At the moment, marriage as it is currently designed is killing relationships - both because it is too much of a sexual, legal and social commitment for most individuals to make for the rest of their lives, and because the fact of being married too often brings about unrealistic assumptions of Happy Ever After in a couple. This lack of realism undermines the requirement for ongoing effort to keep a relationship working, whether it is a marriage or not. Indeed, notions of Happy Ever After just encourage complacency.

If couples make vows for ten years then they are accepting that at the end of ten years both are going to renew their commitment to each other in a total way, or they are going to quit. If both know and accept this then it is much more likely that more couples won't actually quit at ten years but keep going. It will make couples work harder at the relationship, and not take it or each other for granted.

See this as a strategy to ensure longevity in all relationships. People will be much happier in their relationships because they will be more secure and yet also realistic. They will not go into the relationship with the expectation that it will last a lifetime. It may do so, but they cannot take it, or each other, for granted.

2. The Three Identities

One of the hardest lessons we have to learn in life is that no matter whether we are in a relationship or not, we are always on our own. By that I mean we have to follow our own life path, in our own way, making our own decisions as we go. Some of us may well follow this path with a long-term partner beside us, but even so, that partner will have their own path and it won't follow the exact same contours as ours. Many of us are physically on our own anyway, occasionally with a partner, often not. Even so, partner or no partner, our life path is unique to us.

So we have to recognize and accept this reality in relationships, and we have to respect the pathway of our partner. This means not always putting us first, or them. Relationships must be balanced for them to survive, especially in the 21st century. And if a relationship is to have balance it needs to be about sharing rather than giving. Do not imagine just because you love someone that you should give your life for them. The point is for you both to share your lives together, not for one to sacrifice their hopes and aspirations for the other. The hard truth is that there will be times when you need to put yourself first; follow your life pathway very clearly and confidently. Similarly you should never subsume your identity under that of your partner. Nor seek to subsume your partner's identity under yours. You have to allow for the fact that life is fluid and that everything around us is transient. Nothing is permanent. People will come into your life and they will go out of it again, just as you will with others. The first commitment you have is to yourself, your life journey. Follow it, but in a kind, open, honest, and non-hurtful way. Do this and you'll be fine. But if you try to impose on your partner all your own regrets, baggage, recriminations, insecurities, and especially unrealistic expectations, then there is only going to be one outcome and it won't be a long-term loving relationship.

The point here is that there are three elements to every relationship. There is you, there is your partner, and there is the relationship itself. What we have then, are three different dynamics, three different identities. You must appreciate that you and your partner, and all the other aspects of your being together (money, children, home, career, etc.) go to make up the third element: the relationship. This third element has a life and identity of its own, and it too is changing. Don't, therefore, be too egotistical and assume that the relationship is all about you. And don't be too humble and assume the relationship is all about your partner. The relationship itself draws from both of you, and all the other factors going on in your lives, many of which you have little control over.

1. Protect the 3rd Identity: Keep a balance in the relationship by staying on your path and allowing your partner to stay on theirs. Simply do this by following your pathway and allowing your partner to follow theirs. This will create the balance that will ultimately protect the 3rd identity - the relationship. The message here is that you will have to be selfish at times to be a good partner. You must recognize and then accept that you have particular needs and aspirations in your life, so protect them. A good, solid relationship, one that will withstand 21st century pressures, is not built on eternal self-sacrifice, but balanced. You have your own identity, just as your partner does. Long before you make a commitment to any other person you must ensure that your partner fully understands this truth; the truth being that you are each individuals, choosing to come together for as long as possible. But such commitment is based on trust, openness, mutuality, and understanding. It is not based on the assumption that one of you must play second fiddle to the other.

Do not go into a relationship telling yourself that you will put your partner first always, that you will commit fully to him/her whatever, or that you will only consider his/her needs. And don't expect that from him/her. This is the wrong approach. It will just end up backfiring on you. Not only can no one live up to that level of expectation, it leaves you emotionally exposed. The relationship will not thrive if it is out of balance.

2. Recognise Your Relationship Culture: What is the way you do things in your relationship? Every relationship is unique. No two are the same. What emerges in a relationship are patterns of behaviour, attitudes and assumptions about how to be together as a couple. This is the underpinning culture in a relationship and it develops often without the couple being aware of it. This culture comes about from a multitude of major and minor conditions; work roles; family roles; domestic duties; expectations and responsibilities; holiday preferences; how to spend leisure time; when to wake up and when to go to bed; what food to eat; mutual friends; family relationships; a veritable host of things. This relationship culture is one of the glues that will keep a couple together. Just recognize it exists and sense when it is changing or being disrupted.

3. Give it Time: Rome took longer than seven days and so will your relationship. In the beginning of our love affairs all is speeded up, rapid, fast moving and intensely exciting. The world is indeed spinning on its axis and we feel right at the edge of it. But remember this will slow down. Over time, sometimes quite quickly, normality will kick in and you'll be into a predictable routine. This routine is the essence of the relationship for it is out of this that emerges your unique relationship culture (see above). So allow it time to develop. Do not be impatient and certainly do not panic once your world stops spinning. It needs to stop spinning because only then can you begin the real business of being together.

3. Understand Your Love

As I have I described in this book, not only are there are different types of love, love changes over time. Which tells us we need to be able to stand back from our love feelings and recognize what is going on for us. We need to embrace love but in a fuller way and not allow it to delude us into believing the impossible. Love itself does not always bring happiness indeed it can often bring a lot of pain. We must subject our feelings of love to an evaluation. We can understand love by being strong enough to ask questions of it, and at the same time being open to its possibility in our lives.

1. The Love Questions: Do not be afraid to question your love. You do this by asking yourself questions such as; I love this person but do I want to live with him/her? I love this person but do I want to marry him/her? I love this person but do I like his/her character and lifestyle? I love this person but what sacrifices am I prepared to make for him/her? I love this person but what is driving that love, what am I hoping or expecting to get from him/her? I love this person but have I been with him/her long enough to truly know him/her? I love this person but does he/she know me? I love this person but am I really hoping that he/she will change for me?

These are all entirely reasonable questions and you must ask them of yourself whenever you feel love in your life. Do not avoid these questions because they will inevitably emerge at some point. And better to emerge early on in the relationship and get dealt with, rather than later when you are already committed, maybe in marriage.

2. Have No Expectations: None of us knows where our next love comes from so don't go looking for it in specific places. Have no expectations of love, or more precisely, where it might come from. The fact is you have no idea where love might arise next in your life. But for sure it won't arise unless you are open to its possibility. You can find love in the most unlikely, unexpected places, and with the most unexpected people. Disregard issues of appearance, age, beauty, physique, ethnicity; this is just the surface stuff. Love built on the superficial isn't love anyway it just appears to be. And don't confuse romantic gestures with love. Romance can be done highly instrumentally, e.g. with a clear aim in mind. True love is generated through care and attention, not red roses.

3. Be Wary of Virtual Love: Be especially careful with love that develops via email or other virtual communication systems. My research clearly shows that both men and women are very vulnerable to this medium. What happens is that the messages between two people, strangers, intensify in intimacy very quickly. This can take just a week or two. In this period the feeling of love arises and takes hold in you. And in a relatively short time you are 'devoted' to this other person, even though you have yet to meet him/her. I am not saying you shouldn't meet this person. That is not the issue. Just recognize that until you really know this other individual, you are not in love. You are as yet only in love with the feeling of being 'in love.' So keep your emotional distance from any relationship that develops solely through email, for example. Do not say 'I love you' via email or phone until you have met that person and got to know who they are.

4. We All Need A Love Object: Accept that you have love needs to be met, but do not assume they can only be met with another human being. Some of the most content, sorted and happiest people I have ever met live on their own surrounded by cats. Others live on their own with just a Labrador dog for company. One man I know very well is 92, lives alone, but avoids undue feelings of loneliness by looking after his garden and talking to the picture of his deceased wife. His wife is dead but she remains his love object, and a very supportive and important one at that. Whatever your preference, recognize that having a love object will enhance your life. But also, that in the final analysis, after we've tried many human love objects and they've either failed to satisfy or just gone from our lives, then settling down with either an inanimate photo or a very animated pet, might just be what we need.

4. Who is 'The One'?

The core issue in any relationship, whatever type it is, is love. Not necessarily love for another, but love for yourself. You see it is not enough to know yourself. You have to love yourself first before you can truly love someone else or indeed be with someone else in a long-term relationship. Know yourself and love yourself. This is the starting point for any relationship. The answer to the question 'Who is the One?' is you are. Ultimately, there is no one else. There is no other person out there who can replace you or who can give you love if you don't first love and value yourself.

1. You Are Special: Tell yourself this often. Practice telling yourself how special, how lovely and how good you are. Give yourself plenty of positive strokes. Massage your ego. Build yourself up. You need good self-esteem to play the modern relationship game, because if you haven't then you'll just be exposed, vulnerable, and more disappointments will lead to more self-recrimination. It becomes a cycle of declining ego. Get off the cycle as soon as you can. Do not engage in emotional flagellation out of self-pity or self-hatred. No partner can help you if you retreat to such inner anger - in fact just the opposite will occur, because eventually you will transfer your anger focus to that person. At the same time, don't allow your self-esteem to be overwhelming. You are not perfect.

2. Give Something Back: Do good, not bad. If you want to feel good about yourself then it's a good idea to practice giving something good and positive back to this world as often as you can. It can be giving to charity, giving to a complete stranger, doing some good deed for the sake of it, not for any recognition. Do good deeds as often as possible. What goes around comes around. And this action will do wonders for your self-esteem and therefore all your friendships and, of course, relationships.

3. Reflect on Yourself: To know and value yourself requires that you reflect on your actions, emotions and thoughts. Do not rush to self-criticism and don't immediately accept the judgments of others. Be with yourself in a positive way. Think about why things happened in the way they did, what part you had in that, and what you might have done differently. And then move on. Learn from all of it and recognize what you have learned. Look back on the past, and especially past lovers and relationships, with a good heart. And when you look back, see how far you have travelled, reflect on how much you have learned and changed, and see the good in all that. Do not succumb to guilt, regret and anger. Recognise we each have our journey and allow those you love to have theirs. At the end of our time on this earth all we can take with us is what we have learned from life. Let others judge if they want to. You walk with confidence.

5. Learn How To Say Goodbye

Getting into a relationship is usually a whole lot easier than getting out of one. We can become skilled at the former, but rubbish at the latter. We just never learn how to say goodbye. Here are some tips.

1. Timing is Everything: Sense when to leave. Do not attempt to hold on to your good, empowering, relationships long after they have ended. Don't leave a trail of emotional damage behind you.

For sure, you cannot please everyone so don't even try. But you can ensure that an ended relationship has few recriminations and you do this by being open from the outset; you sense when the ending is coming and prepare for it. You do this by recognizing that you have both moved on. It is as simple as that. There is no secret to acquiring a good end to a relationship. You just need to value what you had, value where you each are now, and move on to the new. The aim here is to move the ended relationship into a new friendship. These then become important associations in your life journey. You will reflect on them with a lot of satisfaction. Again, great for your self-esteem. But remember, it takes two to do this, not one

2. Use the 10-year Break-point: This is a built-in get-out point for every relationship. Use it. Recognise that you have given yourself ten years and that now is the time to move on. If you build this into your relationship from the outset then you should be able to leave without recrimination. And follow the 'togetherness vow' that I describe in the final chapter of this book, because this has an ending clause included in it.

3. Accept Change: You cannot avoid change in yourself or your partner. When preparing for leaving think about who you are today, and reflect on how different that person is to the one who started out in the relationship. Likewise your partner should do this also. Neither you nor they may like the changes that have come about, but there can be no argument that they've happened. This is what changed the relationship. Accept it. No one is at fault here. Change happens regardless of our intent.

4. Soulmates Stay Friends: Some people will never leave us. The soulmate love relationship is probably the strongest of all and this will always stay with you long after the other relationships have just become memories. Even if you both go off and have other lovers and marriages, you will always remain soulmates. Stay friends. Keep in contact, get over the disappointment of your relationship ending and allow it to become an important friendship in your life. Always support your soulmate whenever they need it. You may have long ago stopped living with them, but they will never stop being your soulmate.

5. Blame No One: Leaving should be mutual, and even if it is not then it make it that way. Can you imagine going through your life having many relationships and always feeling that you were the one who was hurt and discarded? How painful is that? And how damaging for future relationships when one is totting such recrimination and regret? Too much hurt, too much anger and far too much blame; do not allow it to fester. Best to blame no one. Even if your partner has hurt you badly and acted in such a way as to give you no option but to end the relationship, at least you ended it, not your partner. Or if your partner walks out on you for another lover, then let them go. Do not blame them if they seek happiness elsewhere. That is their choice. It is their love journey. Always look back on what you've learned from these ended relationships. Do not see them as your failure, or that of your partner. Discard the very notion of failure altogether. Real failure comes from not having let go because in that situation you are very likely to take the recrimination into your next love affair.

6. Be Strong Enough to Say Goodbye: Don't get into something you cannot get out of. One of the riskiest relationship scenarios is where a young couple meet, say, at college, start dating and over time come to involve both families and respective friendship groups in a wholesale validation of their relationship. After a while the couple can find it very hard to split, even if they want to. The whole edifice of the relationship gets reinforced and upheld through the expectations of others - especially family. Parents may indeed 'want the best' for their children and see them as happy in their relationship together, when in truth one or both of the partners may well feel they are being swept along on a rising tide of expectation that they will get married and live 'happily ever after'. Basically, you have to be strong in a relationship, even a 'young love' one. It is your life, no one else's. Protect it. Don't be afraid to hurt others if you have to. They will get over it, especially parents. Put at its hardest, do not get married unless you are strong enough to get divorced.

7. Don't force it: Do not create discord in order to bring about a goodbye. You want to leave; you are bored, had enough or just caught up with a new love. This is your issue. So don't transfer it to your partner. All of us can be tempted to create disharmony and fracture in a relationship in order to make it impossible for our partner to stay with us. They just reach their limit and leave, or force us to. Forcing this goodbye is highly manipulative and really hurtful to your partner so avoid doing it. Be strong enough to say your goodbye calmly and reasonably, do not go under cover of war and with an air of pain and hurt around you.

6. Intimacy and Romance

Romance is generally assumed to be the food that feeds a relationship, a critical aspect of togetherness that ensures intimacy and, hopefully, sexual passion. Unfortunately, it is not that simple. It all depends on the intention behind the romantic gesture and type of intimacy that operates in the relationship. Romance can, in fact, contribute to relationship problems. It does this by acting as a smokescreen to what is really going on between two people. This is especially so when 'romantic' gestures have become habitualised; routine, predictable and, therefore, somewhat instrumental. Intimacy cannot be generated through instrumentality it requires spontaneity and unfettered generosity.

1. Don't Play the Romantic Card Too Often: Much better to have an unexpected romantic gesture than one which is just part of an habitualised routine. The flowers at weekends, expensive anniversary dinners, glitzy Christmas cards full of kisses and honeyed words; these can become a problem not a solution. All appears wonderful on the surface while down in the depths real trouble is brewing. We have to be aware that romantic gestures are not always done with pure love intention; they can be done instrumentally and conceal a problem, and therein lies the danger. As one woman said to me: "Yes, he buys me flowers every weekend and never forgets our anniversary, but really what I want is for us to talk more". With romance, the unexpected is much more likely to be remembered than the expected. And if you are going to go away for a romantic weekend, make sure you spend time together sharing, talking, as well as having sex.

2. Intimacy Needs Nurturing: Don't assume intimacy comes with sleeping together. We are in a world where even the supermarket check-out person will flash us a toothy smile and, with apparent sincerity, wish us "have a nice day". However, what she/he really thinks we can only imagine. We are surrounded by a contrived and instrumental intimacy, not a natural one. While this may be acceptable in a supermarket its quite damaging in a relationship. Intimacy needs to be a condition of the relationship but not forced, and this comes about most effectively through sharing moments together. Sleeping together is important but it is not crucial - some of us are chronic snorers. Even sexual relations are not crucial to intimacy. Intimacy comes about from feeling emotionally connected to another person and these moments of connection are most likely to occur when we are listening, looking, paying attention to our partner's words and expressions, sensing their mood and responding appropriately. Intimacy, and romance, can be expressed just through holding hands while out shopping together; that unexpected caress of the face and kiss on the cheek; any expression of genuine care for one's partner. Thoughtfulness and gentleness will, over time, achieve far more than routine sex or predictable anniversary cards.

3: Give Without Expectation: Whatever you give your partner is your gift - don't expect something in return. Romantic gestures and even expressions of intimacy are much better given and received if they are done without expectation of receiving anything back in return. Just give and do so willingly. Find the joy in giving and do not allow feelings of disappointment to accumulate if your partner does not reciprocate. Allow your partner to find their own way of expressing their feelings and love for you

7. Sex

Very few couples can keep the sexual spark going for decade after decade. Some can and they are lucky perhaps in that respect. Most couples can find sexual desire fades away even after a few months, let alone a few years. As I have described in Chapter 5, there are ways of spicing up a sexual relationship and I offer a few. However, there are many other approaches - though this is something a couple can best discover for themselves. The important aspect is being open and honest about one's sexual needs and desires. Start with sexual openness and it is likely to continue throughout the relationship - make it part of your relationship culture. It is much harder to bring such openness in later and after many years of barely concealed disappointment and regret.

1. Sexual Commitment: Monogamy is not for everyone; is it for you and for the rest of your life with the same person? Unless you fully believe that you can be monogamous then do not commit to a relationship expecting to only have sex with that one person for the rest of your life, which in many cases might be for over half a century. Accept this fact and deal with it from the outset, and that means talking openly with your partner about your needs and his/hers. All relationships need to be open like this to some extent. To what extent depends on the couple and is for them to negotiate - but do so frankly and honestly. Do not build your relationship on 'common social expectations' but on the reality of your individual sexual identities and needs.

2. Sexual Honesty: Be clear about your sex needs and distinguish them from your love needs. There are millions of couples around the world that have sex other than with each other and have avoided splitting up as a consequence. This is because they have removed the concept of 'unfaithful' from their relationship contract. They may have been faithful to each other at the beginning of the relationship but over time their individual needs changed and so they adjusted the contract accordingly. The result is they are still together, and love each other more than ever. Remember, there is more than one way to be in a relationship. Find out which way works best for you and your partner.

3. Sex Pain: What do you do if your partner plays away? If you partner reveals that he/she has had sex with someone else, the first question you will ask is 'Who is it?' But this is an ego question, it is not that important. The two most important questions are: 1. Do you love that someone else? 2. Do you want to leave? If the answer to both questions is 'Yes,' then let your partner go. However, if the answer to the first question is 'No,' then do not condemn the relationship to the scrap heap. In my experience, if the first answer is 'No,' then so will be the second one. What we are trying to avoid here is the grief and pain that comes with being 'cheated on' and the subsequent ending of the relationship just because of what is often a casual sexual encounter. The saddest thing is to see an otherwise strong and loving relationship end on the rocks of sexual infidelity. Sexual infidelity on its own should not be enough to finish your love for someone. Give yourselves time to get over the pain and hurt - and reasonable anger. Then move on. Protect your relationship and this you can do if you both truly want to stay together.

4. No Sex Threats: Avoid making demands on your partner that he or she cannot follow through with. For example, many women will tell their male partner that if he has sex with someone else then their relationship is over. This is a control device meant to ensure the man's fidelity. Of course, it rarely works. All the man does is not tell. Which would you prefer: to know or to not know? That is the only question. And only you can answer that. But be aware that if you do impose this condition in the relationship then you have to follow through with it in the event that he is unfaithful. Is this what you truly want? Are you really sure you are prepared to end the relationship over sex? If you are, then what does that say about the type of relationship you are in?

5. Sex and Expectation: We have sex because we enjoy it so make sure your partner is enjoying it also. A full-blooded sexually open relationship will have few if any inhibitions attached to it. Every inhibition acts to limit sexual spontaneity and therefore, sexual pleasure. And pleasure is at the heart of sex; so no inhibitions between the two of you just a mutual desire for exploration and discovery. Not every sexual encounter needs to end in orgasm for both of you, though if one of you is never having an orgasm in your sexual encounters then that is a problem which you should address together. Remember, sex is a mix of the physical and the mental. Good sex can occur without expectation and spontaneously. Good sex can also happen when we are erotically primed for it and have already established an erotic image in our minds long before the actual moment of physical intimacy. So allow both the unexpected and planned to occur. It all adds spice to your sexual menu.

6. Sex and Friendship: Sometimes we need to have sex with our friends just to reinforce our friendship. Many friendships exist in a space between sexuality and companionship. They have a sexual buzz that never entirely goes away. We can be friends with someone yet still feel a sexual curiosity and desire towards them. If both of you feel this then have the sex and then move on to the next stage of your friendship. Often you will find that you have to get the sex out of the way in order to have the truly fulfilling, intimate and nourishing (perhaps non-sexual) friendship that ensues. Sex can provide a friendship with a high level of intimacy and this, in turn, renders it very special. So long as both of you understand what is going on here and talk about it first, then don't let sex get in the way of being friends.

7. Boring Sex: Several years into any relationship and the sex spark is likely to be triggered less and less. Now I accept there are many couples for whom this does not happen but for probably the majority, it does. Sex gets less exciting, more predictable and becomes a habit and routine that while continuing perhaps to be mildly satisfying for one or both partners, is no longer fulfilling in the way it was. Indeed, quite often the sex gets undertaken out of duty, much less out of love. There are ways this might be resolved and I discussed some of the more 'radical' options in Chapter 5, including one or both partners find uncomplicated sex fun elsewhere, at least occasionally. Also, many couples will just accept this situation as inevitable and settle for infrequent predictable sex rather than do anything to upset the relationship itself. However, all is not lost. I recommend the use of sex toys; pornography; new 'naughty' practices such as spanking or bondage; sex drugs such as Viagra, Cialis and Levitra (both men and women can get a rise out of these); and at the very least trying the sex in different places (not just positions) - so sex outdoors, in the kitchen, in the car, even in the garden shed, anywhere but the bedroom. Variety is the essence that spices up the sex - so keep it varied and unpredictable.

8. Honesty

As I have emphasized, no relationship is going to last long without honesty and openness. If these two factors are missing then all you have is the illusion of a relationship; it might look good on the outside but inside it is empty, devoid of true connection.

Nothing will kill a relationship faster and more surely than deceit and dishonesty; these are built around lies that in turn lead to illusion and when one partner sees the illusion exposed then the loss of trust is almost irretrievable. Trust is immensely difficult to overcome once it is has gone. So we have to try and avoid losing it. And being honest with each other is the best way.

1. Do Not Lie: Every lie you tell, even the small ones and those that remain hidden, will eat away at the relationship. From the outset make a pledge to never ever lie to your partner. Be honest even if it means you inadvertently hurt them or yourself. One big issue here is whether or not you should tell your partner if you are unfaithful. Well, of course you should not. If you play away without telling your partner then you have to carry the emotional burden and risk that comes with it, not your partner. Which is fair. But my advice is not to get into that situation in the first place. Much better to let your partner know that you are having feelings of sexual desire outside the relationship before you actual start putting those feelings into practice. A truly open and honest relationship can often deal with these feelings in a mutual way - perhaps by coming to a consensual agreement about extra-marital sex in the way many relationships are, today, doing.

If, however, you conclude that such an open approach is impossible for you and you do embark on a secret affair or occasional sex with others, then you must keep it secret. You must carry the guilt, if any, which comes with it. This is deceitful and it's potentially a major problem, but it is not lying. It is only lying if your partner asks you if you are having an affair - then you must tell the truth. As I say, do not lie. Too many men I have known just cannot hold the guilt of the affair and subsequently tell their wives, hoping to seek forgiveness and absolution. This usually does not happen.

This is why I stress in this book about being open about your sexual needs. I am not countenancing affairs in relationships I am countenancing honesty. But remember, with honesty comes responsibility - your responsibility to be honest and accept honesty from your partner. If one or both of you cannot deal with honesty then the relationship may be able to continue, but only on the basis of illusion.

2. Be Honest About Your Feelings: Like most aspects of a relationship, the starting point is you. Be honest with yourself in a relationship even if in doing so you trigger strong feelings of guilt. For example, be honest about what you expect from your partner and what you can give. Don't act in such a way as to perpetuate the illusion of love. Do not be tempted to hide your true feelings behind romantic gestures; this is a really dangerous type of dishonesty because it creates the illusion of love and permanence when in fact the relationship might already be doomed. If your love for each other is strong then it can be tested. If it fails the test of honesty and transparency, then it is not love, it is 'false love' in which case you know this and can then move on if you wish to. And never ever tell someone you love them just to make them feel good, when you know perfectly well you do not.

9. Communication

No modern relationship can be built on silence. It needs communication between both parties in order to survive and thrive. A strong relationship is strong because both partners are talking to each other, expressing themselves, and listening. The myth of the strong silent type of guy, rugged and reserved, emotionally controlled, is only a movie character. In real life men are not like that. They are highly emotional; it is just that they often do not know how to express their powerful, sometimes overwhelming, emotions in a positive way. They do not learn how to do emotional talk; they do not learn how to reflect on themselves and their feelings. They cannot express their thoughts and concerns productively. But most women can generally do this very well; they talk, and they listen. They hear what is being said and what is not being said. This is where we have the most common mismatch between the sexes.

So what happens when the mismatch erupts? Well, all too often, it can lead to aggression if not violence by the party who is unable to express their deep, strongly felt, inner emotions. And usually this is the man. He will lash out when he cannot find the words to express himself. This is frustration at work. His anger builds up and the more his partner talks and demands he talk to her, the stronger his anger grows. In these situations, when anger is in full flow, and a man says, "That's enough, I don't want to hear any more!" then believe me, he doesn't. That is the time for you to be quiet. Leave the room. Get away from his presence. This is you controlling your feelings, your anger. Leave him so that he can get control over his. Women have admitted to me that they have deliberately provoked their partner in precisely these types of situations. They can see his frustration building and his anger. Perversely they also see this as at least an emotional response from him. And even if it leads to the most awful argument, they reason that such an outburst is better than simmering silence.

Anger management is a very important part of every successful relationship. If anger is constantly erupting, often over the most trivial matters, then for both of you it is a living nightmare, but especially for the person on the receiving end of the anger and frustration. As one woman told me, "It is like walking through an unexploded mine field: you are just so nervous about what to say next because you know it could just touch off a mine and up we go again. I got to the point where I would try and go around smiling all the time, even when I felt miserable. I did this in order to make sure he was happy, and therefore calm."

I say that this is mostly a male issue, but only 'mostly,' and certainly not in every case. Many women too suffer from what I term 'emotional bottling,' where they are constantly on edge of another eruption. One of the main reasons for both men and women suffering from this condition (and it is a condition which can be treated) is that they are angry with themselves. They are disappointed not with their partner so much as with themselves. They are hurting inside, feeling exposed and vulnerable and misunderstood; but that hurt becomes expressed as outward verbal and/or physical aggression towards those nearest and dearest to them.

1. Sometimes a Couple Need Help: Do not feel that you cannot seek outside guidance. Where anger and communication are concerned, a neutral third-party can be a big asset. Chronic anger issues in a relationship need dealing with by a specialist and are beyond the scope of this book. However, be aware that even chronic anger is not a biological problem, it is an environmental one; in other words, people are not born angry, but become that way over time. Unfortunately, chronic anger in a relationship can all too easily become a habitual response to any minor or major difficulty, incident, or problem. It becomes an addictive, almost compulsive response to stress or lack of ability to communicate properly. And as soon as one or both of you are addictively responding this way then the relationship is no longer working productively for either of you. You have to seek outside specialist 'relationship or marriage guidance' help to stop the cycle.

2. Take Time Out: Be calm and provide a calm setting. The fact that anger is invariably not biologically driven is the good news. Because it means that if you spot this anger erupting early on in the relationship then you can try and deal with it early on, not when it is too late. The way you do this is to simply take time out. Let the anger subside. Give each other space to simmer alone. Calmness is the key here. So avoid big discussions about important matters in the relationship when you are tired, stressed, when either or both of you are under the influence of alcohol, or when you are still feeling the effects of your last argument. And when all is calmer, start talking again. But set ground rules for this. And both follow them.

We all need calmness in our life, and in our relationships. Only this way can you really deal with the issues in a rational, reasonable way as and when they surface. The best advice I can give any person who seeks to achieve a deeper calmness in him/herself is to meditate. Just for 5 minutes. Try sitting alone, not thinking of anything in particular. Quieten your mind. Utter silence. Believe me, it works.

3. Stress is Part of Life: Accept that there will be times when you'll both be stressed so prepare for it. Modern relationships have a whole bunch of additional stresses in them that traditional relationships don't have. For example, both of you working full time and trying to hold down a career, maybe raise children, have your own life a little, dealing with financial worries and pressures, while also trying to love each other in a sexually active relationship.

It is asking a lot of both of you!

You both need your own space at times. So be prepared to give it. This might be just going out for a drive on your own; go to the cinema on your own; go out with friends but without your partner; go for a walk alone. Being alone gives you time to reflect and think. Do not fall into the habit of constantly packing your life with activities. We all need time out.

4. Talk and Listen: You may be good at talking but are you good at listening? Listening is fundamental to communication between partners otherwise it is just a one-way verbal wave that has little impact on the other's awareness. Talking can become merely additional noise in our lives if it reduced to a constant torrent of words aimed at our partner. If your partner wants to talk, then you should make the effort to listen and that means allowing them to say what they want to say without interruption. They then should allow you to respond likewise. Balance the communication to ensure its full flow. Do not stifle communication through distance, silence, anger or defensiveness. Listen - you may not like everything you hear but take time out to hear it and to appreciate both the words and the message. And when if you want to talk about something important do so when you are both relaxed, have time together alone, and are not preoccupied with other matters.

10. Perfection

Relationships work best when they are being lived in the real world, not the mythical one. You have a much better chance to make a 'real world' relationship last if neither of you are desperately trying to live an impossible 'perfect' relationship and you can only do this if you both have fully grasped what it takes to live an 'imperfect one.' Trust me, an imperfect relationship is what you will have. The trick is to recognize, accept, and then live with it; make the imperfections work for you both, not destroy the relationship. And you do this by accepting them, not letting them tear you both apart.

Women are often afraid to admit that their relationship is anything but 'perfect.' Similarly, many single women tell me that they would not settle for an 'imperfect' relationship but only want a 'perfect guy'. This is a big problem because it immediately sets up unachievable, unrealistic expectations, not only in the partner but also in themselves.

Why should anyone expect a perfect relationship? Where is that perfection going to come from? From your partner? From you? I doubt it. You would have to be perfect to start with, and I have yet to meet anyone who is perfect. I am sure you haven't met that person either.

So imperfection is the starting point, not perfection.

At the same time, while we are not seeking perfection, we are seeking positive energy from our relationships. That is, we should be with a partner who boosts us, gives us a quiet sense of joy in being with him/her. You don't need to be with your partner every hour of every day, but you like curling up in bed with that person at night, waking up with him/her in the morning. They may not be 'Mr and Miss Right' but your soul smiles when you see them. These are partners who raise our self-esteem not lower it; they make us feel good about ourselves. This is as perfect as it gets.

1. Reflect on the Past: Look for the good in everything and everyone. If it all gets too much sometimes, then just make a note of all your ex-lovers and write down the positives that you got from each relationship. If there were no positives at all (which I very much doubt), then write down what you learned from the experience because for sure you learned something.

2. Ignore Perfection: No one is perfect and all relationships are demanding. You are only giving yourself additional work if you expect anyone or any relationship to be perfect. Some people can accept an imperfect relationship and be in it quite contentedly. Men can be better at this than women. One reason for this is that women tend to make a bigger emotional investment in a relationship and with that investment so too come high expectations. Don't go looking for perfection in anybody. If you want the perfect relationship, get a pet.

3. Love Your Imperfections: Who would want to be with you if you were perfect? If you were perfect you would not only be boringly angelic, you would be impossible to live with. So recognize your imperfections as part of who you are - they are important to your whole character. So long as these imperfections do not become major obstacles to the relationship continuing - e.g. drug, alcohol, or gambling addictions especially - then accept them as elementary to your identity. But then you have to similarly accept and embrace your partner's imperfections.

11. Roles and Responsibilities

All relationships rest on practicalities, indeed the practical and pragmatic are essential to holding people together; these are the building blocks, they create the fabric of a relationship, encourage harmony, signify the trust contract, and over time come to inform the unique culture within which a couple live day by day.

No book can tell you how to do this. It is just impossible to predict. In fact, one of the most exciting aspects of any new relationship is working out and agreeing the ways in which you and your partner will be together. This does not inevitably mean living together, but actually committing yourselves to the important task of 'togetherness', however you both define what that means. Out of this comes the crucial element of 'balance' - the sharing of work and benefits, the sharing of duties and responsibilities, and the sharing of love.

Here are some tips:

1. Decide the Roles: Do not allow others, or tradition, to decide them for you, only you two can do this. In the past, traditional gender roles pretty much decided how a couple would live. That is, husband went out to work while wife stayed at home and raised the family; it is what sociologists call the 'sexual division of labour'. Today, in most developed and developing worlds, and especially amongst the middle classes, such a sexual division of labour is disappearing. So what replaces it? Well, that is up to you two. This is one of the awesome challenges facing all couples in the 21st century - who does what? For some couples this might mean both partners working full-time, both sharing the raising of children and domestic duties. For others it could mean one partner working while the other is the housewife or househusband. If there already are children involved from past relationships then these also need factoring in. If you two decide that a more traditional approach suits you, e.g. man as the main breadwinner, woman responsible for the home and family, then fine. This can work very well indeed. Or you may decide to share everything. That is fine also. What you two eventually come up with is only important for you two. But what is critical is that you mutually agree these roles and responsibilities from the outset.

2.Honour Your Commitments: Each person must fulfill their part of the bargain. Having established and agreed who does what then unless change is necessary, stick to the arrangement. If you cannot be trusted to honour your part of the agreement then you are undermining the trust contract at the heart of the relationship.

3. Write it Down? Do you feel it necessary to declare the roles from the outset? Some couples do indeed write down the duties and responsibilities that each has in the relationship. I think this is fine, but it is not essential. Again, it is up to you two. But my advice is if one partner feels easier having it openly declared and written, then allow it to happen.

5. Change Will Happen: So factor it in. Much as I am espousing the realities of having roles and responsibilities declared from the outset, you need to recognize that change happens and for sure it will happen to you. Unemployment, new career opportunities, financial problems or windfalls, children, parental responsibilities, health issues, these and more can and do impact on most relationships at some stage. This is why I really do encourage open communication between both partners. Only that way can you subsequently address the issues as they arise and, if necessary, renegotiate and revise your roles and responsibilities together.

6. Sharing the Material: love and money don't always go together. In many relationships, especially if there is an imbalance of education and skill, then one person can quickly become the main or sole provider. This also happens if one partner is bringing more 'to the table' than the other. By that I mean, one partner has money and capital, the other very little if anything. Such a material and financial imbalance can easily create insecurity and dissatisfaction between people. One feels always beholden to the other for money and material security, while the person with money feels the pressure to always be the provider and perhaps resentful that the material and the financials aspects of the relationship are not more equally shared. This can only be addressed by communication. Do not assume anything going into the relationship. Those relationships that do not end due to sex often end due to money issues so be prepared for this from the outset. It is vitally important that you both declare your material and financial position if you are going to live together or, indeed, get married. Whatever particular arrangement you agree is, as I stress, up to you two. But discuss it and agree it from the outset. Love crumbles quickly once resentment and jealousy kick in.

7. The Project: The relationship belongs to you both, protect it. Imagine the relationship as an ongoing project that you have both created and duly committed to. It is a project with its own unique energy, character and content, and it belongs to you.

This project lives or dies on the basis of both your involvement in it. There may come at time when one or both of you may decide the project is over. That is your prerogative. But until that day arises you have something to protect and into which you have put a lot of emotional and physical energy. Do not commit to any relationship unless you recognize and accept this reality, and so does your partner.

8. *The Relationship Contract: Every relationship needs clarity, boundaries but also flexibility.* Whether or not you decide as a couple to have your roles and responsibilities written down and clarified, it is a good idea to establish a relationship contract. Many couples do this, though most do it informally. The contract signals the ways you are going to be together, how roles, responsibilities, money and the material wealth are shared, and any number of other factors you choose to include and which are important for you both. I think this is really important and its best to get such a contract established early on in the relationship. At the same time, it is also important to accept that such relationship contracts can change, indeed will need changing or adjusting over time. So like many aspects of being together, flexibility is important. Have the contract certainly, but be strong and wise enough to change it as different needs and circumstances arise.

12. Being On Your Own

Fed up being single, but want to keep your freedom and independence? Decide what it is you want, because you cannot have both. Are you really ready for a full-on relationship or do you just fancy being able to tell your friends that you have someone in your life?' If it's the latter then accept that and treat the relationship for what it is: an adornment. Nothing more. It comes and it goes. It is not a permanent fixture. You put it on when it suits you, and you take it off when you have had enough of it.

Does that sound harsh? Well, perhaps it is. But, frankly, I can see no other way of putting it. Many single people I have met actually like being single. They just don't like not having a relationship. This is the paradox. How to deal with it?

Being single is a state of mind. We can be in a relationship and still feel single in our heads. Many people accomplish this nowadays. It leaves them with a sense of their own individuality, their own freedom, their ability to make choices, especially about whom they date. The trick is to avoid making statements of commitment to your partner. And if he/she persists in wanting such a statement from you, then unless you are prepared to go down that road, forget it. Don't follow his/her lead. Your partner is acting out of insecurity within his/herself, which is your partner's issue, not yours. This is the only way to be single and maintain the sense of independence. Though it cannot work unless your partner is mature and sensitive enough to go along with it. So watch out for partners who lack these qualities.

The truth is, most of us are quite content living on our own, but we also want our sexual desires to be satisfied within a loving relationship. We want sexual and emotional companionship, we just don't want to do the equivalent of trekking the Himalayas to make it work. In these situations you should have what we call a 'peripheral relationship' - that is a relationship that does not define your life, who you are, or your future. This is your choice, it is not that of your partner. But first you have to know what it is you want and what you are prepared to sacrifice to make it work, because you will have to sacrifice something.

1. Can You Make the Commitment? Recognize that big love relationships are hard, they are tough, and they never become entirely easy. If you both want it to last then accept that this will take real effort. And ask yourself these questions: Have you the time to put into a relationship? Have you got other commitments in your life and which come first? Can you bear living with someone day in, day out? Do you like your own space and don't want to give that up for anyone?

These are just some of the questions you must ask yourself. And recognize that how you answer them indicates your actual level of what I call, 'relationship motivation.' If your relationship motivation is primarily driven by not wanting to be seen as a single person in your community, then, as I say, you need a peripheral relationship.

2.Know Yourself: Accept that many of us are just better at being single than being in a couple. All of us need to examine our motivations and expectations. We also need to examine our behaviors and responses. For example, don't harbor unresolved anger and recrimination from previous relationships. These are powerful but negative emotions and they will just hold you back from being able to enjoy love with another person and engage in a fully satisfying relationship. The person who finds it hardest to be in a relationship is often the same person who finds almost impossible to reflect on their attitudes and behaviours. Such individuals really are better at being single than in a couple.

3. Keep Sex Separate: Don't confuse desire for a regular and steady sexual relationship with a desire to be in 'coupledom.' Recognize and accept your needs, don't feel guilty about having them, and be honest not only with yourself but also your partner. Open communication here is vital to prolonging the relationship. If you just want occasional sex and good companionship then make that clear from the outset. Don't tumble unwittingly into a heavy relationship when in truth that is not what you are seeking.

4. Try A Relationship Sabbatical: We all need to replenish our emotional energies at times and a good way to do this is to be alone for a spell. If you are in a relationship but have strong feelings of wanting to be single, at least some of the time, then try what I call a 'relationship sabbatical.' Take time out from each other. Give yourselves time to re-evaluate what you want and see if this absence rekindles the spark and motivation. If it doesn't, then you know you've come to the end of the road, if it does, then fine. How long should a sabbatical be? Well you both need time on your own, and away from each other. Perhaps not at the beginning of the relationship, but many couples come to this realization eventually. It could just be a few nights away each month, or it could be much longer. But talk about it first. Don't do what many couples do and just inadvertently slip into increasingly prolonged absences without first discussing why you are doing it. That way leads to permanent absence. And one more thing, you never pry too much into what your partner gets up to during these 'sabbaticals.' If he/she wants to tell you, then fine. If not, that is their choice. If you are the sort of person who needs to be with their partner 24/7 and cannot let them out of your sight for more than an hour or so without fretting about what they are up to, then stick to being single.

13. Happiness and Contentment

Happiness is not a constitutional right. Nor is it a relationship right. Happiness is something that comes from within us, not from outside us. If you do not emit happiness to others then it is unlikely you'll receive much in return. Also we need to be content to even get close to being truly happy. Contentment is the starting point for happiness, not the other way round. And contentment is an internal feeling. Below are some philosophical perspectives on happiness and contentment.

1. Happy Today? If you are not happy today then what makes you think you will be happy tomorrow? By thinking you'll be happy tomorrow you are just delaying the arrival of the happiness you yearn for. Be content in the moment, not in hopes for the future.

2. State of Mind: Neither lasting happiness nor deep contentment will come from external elements, e.g. drink, drugs, sex or money. These may give you some pleasure and intermittent satisfaction, but in themselves they will not make you happy. Some of the happiest and most content people I have ever met are male and female monks living highly frugal and spiritual lives in temples.

3. Positive not Negative: Always be positive about your life as it is and what is coming up next. I know this can be incredibly difficult at times, but being positive is a state of mind that can really strengthen a relationship. Similarly, be optimistic rather than pessimistic - life is ultimately short but also very special. The fact you are here at all is a miracle in itself.

4. Some Things Don't Get Sorted: Accept that not every problem you face will get resolved. Some things you just have to let go of and allow them to be. They will go away or not. Certainly over time they can become less important. Some problems we just have to live with.

4. Accept Karma: You may not call it karma - I actually perceive it as life balance. In other words, what goes around comes around. Sometimes life will be painful but that is nothing new. Sometimes it will be joyous. That is to be expected also. Whatever comes along, accept it as karma, life balance. I think The Beatles lyrics from their *Abbey Road* LP are particular apt here; "In the end, the love we make is equal to the love we take".

5. Avoid Displacement: To be in an empowering love relationship takes commitment. It requires togetherness. Displacement can arise when we put more effort into our careers, for example, than our love life. In such situations, the work organisation or our professional position assumes too great a hold over our identity, our sense of who we are, and our sense of worth. This is a seductive trap for all of us. However, while it can give you some contentment, remember, no work organisation is going to love you more than your soulmate.

6. *Self-sufficiency:* Don't get into relationships simply because you are afraid of being on your own. Learn to be self-sufficient because then you'll know that you can be on your own if you have to be. Being self-sufficient is not just about being able to earn a living and live an independent lifestyle, it is about being emotionally independent also; sorted in yourself and comfortable in your skin.

Chapter 7: Manifesto Rules

Relationship Vows for the 21st Century

"The promise given was a necessity of the past: the word broken is a necessity of the present." (Niccolo Machiaveli)

In this final chapter I summarise the core truths to all relationships and offer what I consider to be the key relationship vows that any couple can make to each other. The core truths are presented first because, in my opinion, these frame the reality for all relationships and, therefore, for all relationship vows.

Machiavelli is right of course in respect of human behaviour - all is ultimately expedient, not least our promises to be faithful and love forever. It is just too easy to say "I will love you for the rest of my life'. In truth this statement is meaningless. We cannot possibly know what life holds for us or indeed, how we will feel about someone years down the line. As Machiavelli warns, ultimately we have to deal with the necessity of the present, not the promise of the past. The 'love vow' is a problem because we read so much into it and assume so much from it. It becomes a screen behind which all types of relationship issues emerge and fester over time. In believing in the veracity of the love vow so we fail to heed the critical everyday lived vows - yet these are the vows which will determine whether the relationship lasts or not. As I say, love vows won't hold it all together if the very fabric of the relationship is rotting away. Which is why I have deliberately removed the word 'love' from the relationship vows offered below. If you wish to insert it, that is your right. But be aware of the unpredictability at the heart of relationships, and at the heart of love.

We need vows that are achievable in the light of the relationship reality now manifestly apparent at this point in the 21st century.

At the same time, we need vows that signal to us the importance and responsibility that come with a committed relationship. Such vows are offered to you below. You may consider them ideal for your needs. Or you may consider them more useful as guidelines. If the latter, then as a couple, one of the first projects you can undertake together is to agree and write down your own vows for your own unique relationship. And then speak them; publicly or not, it is up to you.

The mere act of having to agree your vows together will in itself instill in you both a powerful recognition of the seriousness of the commitment you are getting into.

If you can agree your vows, then you are at least in a position to try living them out.

The Core Truths

1. *There is no such thing as permanent. Everything is impermanent, changeable, fluid. Including you and your partner.*

2. *Every relationship gets tested. There is no escape from this. Even the easier, peripheral relationships will test you both at times. Accept that there will be periods when you feel lost, confused, hurt and in pain. But remember, this is not just true of relationships it is true of life itself.*

3. *If you are in a relationship that is central to you, vitally important and to which you*

have made a commitment, then do not waver. Do not be flaky when times are tough. Keep your standpoint, which is that the relationship needs to last. You must face your tests together.

4. *Your life is a journey that only you can experience. People will come into your life and share important aspects of it with you at different times. But ultimately, it is your journey.*

5. *No relationship will survive if only one person is doing the emotional labour. It takes two.*

6. *See each problem as an opportunity to build your relationship even stronger. You overcome your problems together. In this way so will your bond with your partner strengthen. Love won't hold a relationship together, only bonding can do that and bonded relationships are built through balance, communication, respect and honesty.*

7. *Don't be hung up by sex. Recognise sex as a fundamental aspect of the human condition and not one that can be boxed in through moral codes. Affairs are damaging but they need not be fatal. Honesty is the key here. If your partner tells you they have had an affair but want to keep the relationship with you, then do everything possible to continue.*

8. *When it comes to relationships, remove the word 'failure' from your vocabulary. No relationship is a total failure for the simple reason that we learn from all of them. You do not have failed relationships you have had relationships that have ended, come to their natural conclusion.*

9. *You are in love? Then reflect on what that means for you and what you expect from this love, what you are prepared to give and what you are expecting to receive.*

10. *Grow together, share together, but stay true to yourself. Recognise, accept and love the person you are.*

Relationship Vows

These are tough vows to make and even tougher vows to keep. So don't underestimate them. But if you can keep to them then you'll have a relationship that is perfect as it gets. Mutual love can still be the foundation, but your togetherness gets bonded through these vows not through promises of 'eternal love'.

I promise to do everything in my power to keep our relationship together for the next 10 years.

I promise to renew our relationship vows in ten years time but only if I am sure I can make that commitment.

I promise to be honest and open with you in respect of my sexual needs and desires.

I promise to listen to your needs and concerns calmly and respectfully.

I promise to fulfill the relationship role and responsibilities that we have agreed I should undertake so long as I am physically and mentally able.

I promise to respect you and treat you with respect at all times.

I promise not to take any lifestyle, career or financial decisions that might affect our relationship without consulting with you first.

I promise to care for you to the best of my ability should you ever be ill, infirm or incapacitated.

I promise not to abuse you emotionally or physically.

I promise to put our relationship first in my life for the next ten years.

I promise to seek your consent before embarking on sexual relations with any other person.

I promise to respect your religion or belief system even if it is not my own.

I promise not to impose my own religion or belief system on you.

I promise to come to you if and when I am unhappy or unsettled in our relationship.

I promise that you can always come to me if you are ever unhappy or unsettled in our relationship or with any other aspect of your life.

Glossary

Bi-sexuality: The ability of a person to enjoy sex with both men and women.

Compulsory Heterosexuality: The assumption that only heterosexuality is normal and therefore that LGBT sexualities/identities are abnormal and unnatural. Once this assumption takes hold in a society then social pressure arises to present oneself as only ever heterosexual.

Displacement: This usually arises when we are fearful or uneasy about a situation or person and rather than engage with it/them we instead engage in those activities that take us away from such a connection. For example, spending increasing amounts of time at work rather than at home, or alone rather than with our partner.

Emotional Dysfunctionality: Within a relationship this takes the form of an inability to engage emotionally with a partner or lover; to be fearful of expressions of emotion and empathy; the attempt at constant self-control of one's emotions; the desire to hide one's feelings and emotions and not express them openly and freely; the inability to be reflexive and emotionally self-aware. May also be referred to as 'Emotional Distancing'.

Emotional Labour: The acts and practices that significantly contribute to sustaining a positive emotional presence and validity within a relationship and which in turn assist in cementing the emotional, physical and intimate bond between a couple.

Femininity: Those behaviours, attitudes, practices and performances of identity that a society or culture associates only with women and therefore assumes to be the natural properties of womanhood and women's gender and sexuality. Operates in opposition to masculinity.

Gay: Overall term which includes men who enjoy sex with men (msm) and men who adopt the label 'gay' as a (political) expression of their gender and sexual identity.

Gender Binary: The belief that society is inherently and naturally structured around men (masculinity) and women (femininity) and that both gender and sex operate through distinct and biologically given dualisms; e.g. gay-straight; active-passive; strong-weak; masculine-feminine; manly-effeminate.

Gender Discourses: Dominant and subordinate ways of being a man or a woman, gay or straight, and ways of talking and thinking about men and women, straight and LGBT people within specific social and cultural settings.

Gender Identity: The performances of individuals that reflect either or both male and female, masculine and feminine, identities. Such performances are social expressions, not biologically driven. They have the potential to either reinforce or challenge dominant assumptions around maleness and femaleness. Gender is usually seen as the social expression of sex identity.

Intersexed: A physical condition wherein the individual has indeterminate genitalia, that is, they are neither self-evidently male or female. With intersexed babies, it is now considered best not to 'decide' which sex they are at birth, but to allow them to discover their 'natural' sex/gender identity from puberty onwards.

Hegemonic Masculinity: A dominant and persuasive attitude within a society or culture that encourages and privileges a way of being a man that purports to be physically strong, straight, homophobic, aggressive, assertive, emotionally controlled, macho, avoiding and dismissive of feminine displays; privileges men over women and straights over gays; and sexually predatory.

Karma: The belief that the actions we do in this life, and have done in past lives, will have an effect on our lives in the future. That is, if we do good deeds then good deeds will return to us, and if we do bad deeds then so will bad deeds also return to us. Ideas of karma are especially apparent in Buddhism and Hinduism.

Ladyboys (also known as Kathoey, or the 'third sex', in Southeast Asia): Individuals born male but who come to present themselves as female and overtly feminine from puberty onwards as this feels, for them, their 'natural' gender/sex. Most ladyboys/ kathoey will have hormone replacement therapy from puberty and thereby acquire breasts and other physical expressions of femininity. A few will undergo full genital-reassignment surgery.

LATS ('living aparts togethers'): Couples, either gay or straight, who although in a committed relationship, decide not to live together but to continue with their individual domestic arrangements. Invariably this means living apart while being together emotionally and intimately.

Lesbian: Overall term which includes women who enjoy sex with women (wsw) and women who adopt the label 'lesbian' as a (political) expression of their gender and sexual identity.

LGBT: Lesbian, Gay, Bisexual and Transgendered persons.

Life Balance: Refers to ensuring one's life is full but not overwhelmed by a single aspect or situation. So aiming, for example, to achieve a balance in terms of work and leisure, physical activity and rest, stimulation and relaxation, emotional commitment to another and emotional commitment to oneself.

Masculinity: Those behaviours, attitudes, practices and performances of identity that a society or culture associates only with men and therefore assumes to be the natural properties of manhood and men's gender and sexuality. Operates in opposition to femininity.

Matriarchy: A prevailing condition within a society, culture or local setting (e.g. a family) whereby women come to be the dominant, privileged and most powerful sex.

Monogamy: Relationships (both casual short-term and committed long-term) that do not permit or accept more than one sexual partner and therefore operate strictly within the confines of coupledom (two people).

Patriarchy: A prevailing condition within a society, culture or local setting (e.g. a family) whereby men come to be the dominant, privileged and most powerful sex.

Polyamory: A consensual arrangement between two people (usually sexual partners), that permits both to engage with sexual encounters with others outside the relationship. Different polyamorous couples may well construct different contracts and specific conditions for this arrangement.

Polygamy: A marriage in which one or both of the partners has another wife or husband. For example, in those societies where polygamy is legal, a husband may be allowed two or more wives.

Postmodern Man/Woman: Men and women who do not normally conform to traditional expressions and notions of masculinity and femininity but who choose to present themselves in a more fluid and open way, both in terms of their gender identity and sexuality.

Prostitution: An overall term that encompasses every aspect the sale/exchange of sex for money/material reward. This includes professional sex work, sex tourism, escorting, child sex, sex trafficking, opportunistic and occasional sex work.

Sexual Dysfunctionality: The inability to perform the sex act within a relationship. The reasons for this may be physical (e.g. inability to get an erection) and/or mental (e.g. loss of libido and general lack of desire for sex).

Sex Identity: Invariably the male or female identity imposed on individuals at birth and which corresponds to the presence of either a penis or a vagina.

Sex/Gender Roles: The roles which a society or culture considers most natural or appropriate for men and for women; e.g. women as carers and housewives, men as breadwinners and earners. These roles have traditionally and in the past, been associated with the male-dominated public sphere of work and the female-dominated private sphere of the home. Also links to the concept of a 'sexual division of labour'.

Sex Work: The profession of sex working and act of sex work, in which a man or woman chooses to become a sex worker for material gain and subsequently performs the roles and requirements of this work in a professional and fully renumerated context.

Swinging: Usually associated with anonymous group sex in which a combination of straight, gay, lesbian or bisexual acts may occur. Swinging may take place in either a designated club or in the privacy of a home.

Transgendered: A state of being in which the individual consistently performs a gender identity contrary to the one they were assigned at birth. In this state the individual has not undergone full genital reassignment.

Transexual: A physical and emotional condition in which the individual has fully crossed over to the opposite sex their were assigned at birth and has this new sex identity confirmed through full genital reassignment surgery. In those countries where transexuality is legal, the individual may be able to have their new sex identity validated through a passport and other legal mechanisms.

Indicative Bibliography

Other books by Stephen Whitehead:

Whitehead, S., Talahite, A., and Moodley, R. (2013) *Gender and Identity: Key Themes and New Directions:* Oxford: Oxford University Press

Whitehead, S. and McNicol, R. (2011) *16 Faces of Women: London: Andrews* *

Whitehead, S. (2010) *Men, Women, Love and Romance: Under the covers of the bedroom revolution.* London: Andrews *

Whitehead, S. (ed) (2006) *Men and Masculinities: Critical Concepts in Sociology (Volumes 1,2, 3, 4, 5).* London: Routledge

Whitehead, S. (2004) *The Many Faces of Men.* London: Arrow

Whitehead, S. (2002) *Men and Masculinities: Key Themes and New Directions:* Cambridge: Polity.

Whitehead, S. and Barrett, F. (eds) (2002) *The Masculinities Reader.* Cambridge: Polity.

Dent, M. and Whitehead, S. (2001) *Managing Professional Identities: Knowledge, Performativity and the 'New' Professional.* London: Routledge. *

Whitehead, S. and Moodley, R. (eds) (1999) *Transforming Managers: Gendering Change in the Public Sector.* London: Taylor and Francis. *

* Also available as ebook and ibook versions.

Additional recommended readings:

Adler, N. J. (2002) *International Dimensions of Organizational Behaviour.* London: Thomson

Beasley, C. (2005) *Gender and Sexuality: Critical Theories, Critical Thinkers.* London: Sage.

Bernstein, R. (2009) *The East, The West, and Sex: A History of Erotic Encounters.* New York: Knopf.

Coad, D. (2008) *The Metrosexual.* New York: New York State University

Easton D. and Hardy, J. W. (2009) *The Ethical Slut.* New York: Celestial Arts.

Gherardi, S. (1995) *Gender, Symbolism and Organizational Cultures.* Thousand Oaks: Sage.

Hakim, C. (2012) *The New Rules of Marriage.* London: Gibson Square Books.

Halberstam, J. (1998) *Female Masculinity.* Durham: Duke University Press

Haywood C. and Mac an Ghaill, M. (2003) *Men and Masculinities:* Buckingham: Open

University Press.

Kessler, S. J. (1998) *Lessons from the Intersexed.* New York: Rutgers University Press.

Kimmel, M. S., Hearn, J. R. and Connell, R. W. (eds) (2004) *Handbook of Studies on Men and Masculinities.* Thousand Oaks: Sage.

Meen, D. T., Gibson, M. A. and Alexander, J. F. (2010) *Finding Out: An Introduction to LGBT Studies.* Thousand Oaks: Sage.

Morrison, E. (2008) *Swung.* London: Vintage

Prasso, S. (2006) *The Asian Mystique.* New York: Public Affairs.

Richardson, D. and Robinson, V. (eds) (2008) *Introducing Gender and Women's Studies.* London: Palgrave.

Ryan, C. and Jetha, C. (2012) *Sex At Dawn.* New York: Harper Perennial.

Salih, S. and Butler, J. (eds) (2004) *The Judith Butler Reader.* New York: Blackwell.

Taormino, T. (2008) *Opening Up: A Guide to Polyamory.* New York: Cleis Press.

Woodward, K. (ed) (1997) *Identity and Difference.* London: Sage

Lightning Source UK Ltd.
Milton Keynes UK
UKHW012300070223
416610UK00001B/248